Southampton's
Children of the Blitz

above: Stunned Southampton residents inspect Above Bar after a bombing raid in March 1941.

Southampton's
Children of the Blitz

Andrew Bissell

For James and David

First published in 2001 by
Red Post Books
Reprinted 2004
© Red Post Books 2001/2004
Re-issued by Centenar Publishers 2010
© Centenar Publishers 2010

Designed and produced by Crispin Goodall Design

Printed and bound in the United Kingdom by
the MPG Books Group

A CIP catalogue record for this book is available from
the British Library.

ISBN 978-1-907680-01-4

Centenar Publishing
70 Broughton Avenue
Bournemouth
BH10 6JA
www.centenar.co.uk

Telephone +44 (0) 1202 252144
email: crispin@crispingoodall.co.uk

Centenar publishes illustrated non-fiction books. If
you have a title which you think may be of interest,
we would be pleased to hear from you. You should
address your enquiry to the Editorial Director at the
above address.

Contents

Acknowledgements

My first debt of thanks is to the contributors who so kindly allowed me to use their testimonies in this book. I will never forget their generosity, hospitality and willingness to assist even though many were recalling painful personal memories. These marvellous people became my research team and this work would not have been possible without them.

Certain individuals deserve special mention. Sincere thanks go to local historians Mr Jon Honeysett, Mr Maurice Young and Mr Harry Griffiths for their support, advice and encouragement. Their meticulous approach to research was inspirational and their sheer enthusiasm for this project more important than they probably realise. I am also particularly grateful to: The Mary Evans Picture Library (The Weimar Archive), London; Mrs Sue Woolgar and her team at Southampton Archives Services in Southampton; Janice Mullin at the Photograph Archive of the Imperial War Museum, London; Southampton City Council; Mr Ian Murray, Editor of the Southern Daily Echo, Southampton; Mr Paul Collins and his photographic team at the Southern Daily Echo; Mr Keith Hamilton, Assistant Editor at the Southern Daily Echo, for his valued advice; Mr

Andy Puntis, graphic designer at the Southern Daily Echo, for his contribution of maps for the project; Mr Ian Abrahams and the Bitterne Local History Society, Southampton; and Squadron Leader Alan Jones, MBE, and his staff at the R J Mitchell Memorial Museum Ltd in Southampton.

Every effort has been made to acknowledge the ownership of the copyrighted material included in this book and the following are thanked for allowing me access and use of their photographic archives: The Imperial War Museum, London; The Southern Daily Echo, Southampton; Rolls Royce PLC and The Daily Echo, Bournemouth.

I have also received substantial help, encouragement and support from my publishers, Crispin Goodall and Roger Guttridge. I sincerely thank them both for ensuring the draft included at least the basics of the English language and a modicum of correct grammar. I would also like to thank my family. My parents Molly and Eric have given me a love of history and nearly four decades of encouragement; and, most important of all, my wife Jill and sons James and David have given me ceaseless love and support.

Andrew Bissell.

left: **German merchant seamen in Southampton leaving for prisoner of war camps**.

INTRODUCTION

A personal prologue

I STOOD and watched. A child with inflated jacket, huge luminous training shoes and silver scooter first flashed past the spot I had come to see. Next a family waddled by with bulging Debenhams bags, forcing oncoming human traffic to make a detour. Then a large group of children passed, a chattering huddle of stripy Saints football shirts. Now couples engrossed in each other's company. Not one person stopped to inspect the small stone block at their feet. Not a glance. Not the slightest flicker of acknowledgement.

I walked down Houndwell Place to inspect it for myself. There, inscribed on the side of the rectangular slab, were the words:

"DURING THE SECOND WORLD WAR, SOUTHAMPTON SUFFERED A SERIES OF AIR RAIDS IN WHICH 631 PEOPLE WERE KILLED AND OVER TWO THOUSAND INJURED. IN NOVEMBER 1940, A PUBLIC SHELTER IN THIS PARK RECEIVED A DIRECT HIT IN ONE OF THE HEAVIEST NIGHTS OF BOMBING ENDURED BY THE CITY."

Today the little plaque goes unnoticed. The hustle and bustle of city life swirls past seemingly oblivious to its existence, let alone its significance. There is a similar memorial inside the entrance to Ocean Village. Another is fixed near the ground in Spitfire Walk, Woolston. A more elaborate monument, a small decorated room in fact, can be found within the labyrinthine Civic Centre complex. Then there's the towering stone Cenotaph in Watts Park dedicated to "the men, women and children of Southampton".

They are all reminders of the "Blitz" tragedy and testament to the fact that human imbecility and savagery knows no bounds. Yet they also exist in a peculiar time warp. They are reminders of the past sitting in the present and time has mischievously blurred the connection. They therefore remain physically present but somehow divorced from modern day relevance.

Memorials are created in one environment with a set of meanings contemporaries understand and they matter deeply to those who created them. Those who follow inherit the earlier meanings but also add new ones of their own. By the time the third generation arrives, any meaning has almost faded and these structures cease to be active sites of memory.

Hence these once special places are today in danger of simply merging into the cityscape background where passing, scanning eyes fleetingly see them but particular interest is rarely registered to the brain. It's no-one's fault. No-one is to blame. There is no conscious, collective turning of a blind eye. Time simply moves on. People live for the present and senses are tuned accordingly.

I have never heard the whistle of dropping bombs; I have never spent endless hours in a damp, cold air raid

shelter; and I have never emerged to see streets of fire and mutilation.

Nonetheless, I found myself saddened to see modern life progress so independently of past life that day in Houndwell Place.

My feelings were curious to comprehend since I have no particular affiliation or association with Southampton, its people or its history. I was actually born and raised in the London Borough of Sutton and my journalistic travels have until recently steered me clear of Southampton. However, since becoming a working journalist in the city, I have found myself increasingly drawn to the catastrophe which descended in 1940. It was a lure which I suspect was subconsciously influenced by my father's vivid recollections of the Blitz during his East London childhood.

I now found myself wanting to remind people of what happened in Southampton. Of course, there are those who believe the whole notion of "war remembrance" should be jettisoned and the dead allowed to rest in peace. I strongly disagree. Only rootless, selfish, short-sighted societies decide to forget the past and choose not to profit from experience. I believe it is our collective

and individual duty to remember and ensure that those who follow do the same.

It may be trendy in the sound bite twenty-first century to be proudly ignorant of the past. It is also, in my opinion, profoundly dangerous for society. It was these jumbled views, influences and observations that prompted me to write this book. I wanted, on one level, to revive interest and understanding in Southampton's darkest hour with an unashamedly populist and accessible account; I also wanted, without being insultingly pompous, to reach a new generation with the story; and finally, after meeting so many Blitz survivors, I wanted to ensure that the flickering memories of sacrifices made were not extinguished forever.

This book is primarily offered as an additional contribution to the oral history of the period. Eighty people were interviewed to enable me to colour the canvas and provide the backdrop and a number of key contributors then helped apply the finer details. The children of the Blitz are not getting any younger and there will inevitably come a time when such accounts die with their owners. Their stories will become enveloped by the mists of time and invention,

9

exaggeration and even untruths will make their claim. This book is therefore largely devoted to eyewitness accounts and the words of these key,
contemporary contributors appear in italics to emphasise their importance.

Equally, I have attempted to weave the new first person stories within the complex tapestry which made up the backdrop of the times. The result is a chronological ordering of the material from 1939-45 which, I hope, offers the reader a degree of interpretation and analysis of the wider events which influenced Southampton's ordeal.

Finally, an additional explanation of terminology, timescale and the overall plot may be useful. The German word "blitz" means "lightning". Its first appearance in the vocabulary of war was as part of the phrase "Blitzkrieg", meaning "lightning war", which saw fast moving tanks and armoured divisions smashing through front lines supported by synchronised attacks by Luftwaffe (German Air Force) dive-bombers. The Nazi Blitzkrieg thus spread through Poland, the Low Countries and France before Hitler's legions stared across the Channel and contemplated the next tasty morsel: Great Britain. In 1940 the term was adopted in Britain though here it was strangely stripped of the syllable which actually made any sense of it. Blitzkrieg therefore remained a foreign word but "blitz" became a household term applied to a bewildering range of expressions in the decades that followed. However, when used with a capital letter, the word Blitz will always be associated with 1940. The Blitz itself was part of the Battle of Britain during which Hitler attempted to implement the invasion of these isles with Operation Sea Lion. Hitler set aerial supremacy over the Royal Air Force (RAF) as a prerequisite to land invasion and the classic conflict in the skies raged over southern England from July 10 until September 17, 1940 when Hitler postponed Operation Sea Lion indefinitely. This was the aerial combat phase of the Battle of Britain.

Next came the "Blitz", a bombing war of attrition and one that laid waste vast areas of Britain's major ports, towns and cities. The bombing of towns and cities including Southampton had occurred before and during the aerial combat phase of the Battle of Britain but the classic "Blitz period" really began with the first major raid on London on September 7, 1940. It then continued way beyond the usually defined end date for the Battle of Britain – October 31, 1940 – when intensive night raids stopped. Indeed, in Southampton the bombing attacks didn't reach their devastating climax until November 1940 and continued (in line with national experiences) until mid-1941 and beyond. Meanwhile, the London "finale" was on Saturday May 10, 1941 when 1,400 were killed during a five-hour ordeal.

The Blitz was a national calamity. The ordeal of Southampton and London was, for example, shared to varying degrees by Belfast, Birmingham, Bristol, Liverpool, Manchester, Nottingham, Cardiff, Coventry, Glasgow-Clydeside, Newcastle-Tyneside, Hull, Plymouth, Portsmouth and Sheffield.

This book is about the experiences of Southampton which in the text is referred to as a "town" since city status was not conferred until 1964. The main players who determined the destinies of nations are not the essential focus of this volume. It is not primarily about the brilliance of exceptional individuals who planned, underpinned and ultimately secured Britain's Finest Hour. What it is about is the experience of everyday people – particularly children – whose innocent lives collided with the brutal and ferocious firepower spawned by megalomania. It's a story of ordinary people who were forced to confront and endure extraordinary hardship. The accounts are invariably moving, sometimes harrowing and frequently inspirational.

This, then, is the story of the Blitz children. It is also my respectful tribute to them.

Andrew Bissell.

CHAPTER 1

Jean's Great Escape

A town prepares for terror, 1939 – July 1940

JEAN knew it was now or never. There was no turning back. Early that afternoon she slipped unnoticed out of the house and embarked upon the great escape. Soon shae was running, her 11-year-old legs pumping like tiny pistons down the street.

Jean had left her sister behind but there, at the secret rendezvous, three young fellow escapees were waiting. Now the intrepid band, clutching sandwiches for the epic journey, began their walk to freedom and home. It would, insisted Jean, be simple. They would leave Christchurch, the town which had been their prison, and head for the New Forest. There they would make friends with the New Forest ponies and ride home triumphant to Southampton.

As the great trek began, the experiences of the past few months filled Jean's head. She had never wanted to come to Christchurch in the first place. It was her mum who had said she would be safe there from the bombers. Safe from that strange little man called Adolf Hitler who might try and blow up their Southampton home. Yes, it would be best if she went to stay in the country. Besides, she could always see Mummy and Daddy at weekends. Yet it had been a nightmare.

Acute, churning anxiety had engulfed Jean and many of her Foundry Lane School friends when they left Southampton's Terminus Terrace Station

left: **Jean Thorn** (with hand to neck) surrounded by friends and neighbours.

with large chunks of chocolate, nervous smiles and the prospect of an uncertain future. Christchurch was their destination but Jean's younger brother James ended up on one side of the town while she and elder sister Ivy were greeted by an elderly couple on the other.

When Jean and Ivy entered the terraced house, they stepped back in time. The youngsters swept through the gloomy interior, past the old fire range and then up to their bedroom with its walls covered with photographs of the owners' sons killed in the Great War. The

below: **Adolf Hitler.**

eyes of the heroes followed them around the room, studying, analysing, mulling over the room's new inhabitants, daring them to put a foot wrong.

The couple's married daughter also lived at the house with her children. Segregation was soon introduced at mealtimes and the two young evacuees ate in the kitchen while the daughter's children sat in the relative comfort of the dining room. Then there were the chores: digging potatoes, creosoting the fence, the constant, backbreaking scrubbing and cleaning. The daughter's children did nothing but smile behind their mother as she shouted orders at the newcomers.

Loneliness and isolation befriended Jean and Ivy too. They were silent, cold forces which sneaked upon them at night and reduced them to tears beneath the sheets. All that was in the past now. The New Forest beckoned — and a date with the magical ponies. Or so Jean thought.

A car appeared, its driver peering over the steering wheel with eyes fixed on them. He looked a rather official, stuffy type. Someone important. The car slowed to a halt and the window lowered. The motorist leant out and told the runaways to get home before driving on. A little later the car appeared again as it made its return journey. The runaways immediately dived into a ditch, hearts thumping and pulses racing. After what seemed

an eternity they ventured out — only to discover the man standing before them, his hands on his hips.

Now he was asking difficult questions. He was barring the way. They were in big trouble. The youngsters spilled the beans and the man, a civil servant, drove them to a police station where the questioning would continue. The escape plot, the children's bid for freedom, had failed after just three hours. One of the girls was now so frightened that she wet herself on the back seat of the car.

Young Jean Thorn and her accomplices had been evacuated from Southampton the day before Britain declared war on Germany. It had been a precaution. A move for the best while the world held its breath and prepared for the unimaginable. As early as November 1938, the government had begun making

above: **Foundry Lane School, Southampton.**

left: **Foundry Lane School class with Jean Thorn in second row, second from right. Many of the school's children were evacuated to Christchurch.**

evacuation plans to use in the event of war. Conflict was not inevitable then. There was still a faint glimmer of hope. On September 30, 1938, the craggy features of 70-year-old Prime Minister Neville Chamberlain had beamed before a large crowd upon his return from a meeting with Adolf Hitler in Munich. As he stepped from the plane at Heston aerodrome in Middlesex, he lifted a frail arm to wave a piece of paper he was carrying. "I've got it," he cried before being whisked off to Downing Street where more crowds awaited.

At Number 10 he said the words which were to haunt him for the remainder of his life: "This is the second time that there has come back from Germany to Downing Street peace with honour. I believe it is peace for our time." How they cheered. How they clapped. In a nearby building, the eyes of the man who would one day become Chamberlain's successor, Winston Churchill, filled with tears. He knew war was imminent. The "Gathering Storm", as he called it, was approaching.

It was not long before Hitler, Germany's beloved "Fuehrer" or leader, placed the last piece of the tragic jigsaw in place. When his tanks rolled across the Polish border in the early hours of September 1, 1939, Europe careered into a violent maelstrom which would claim the lives of some 55 million people – two thirds of them civilians.

On the same day, sleepy children rubbed their eyes and climbed from their beds and prepared to leave home. Some would never see their homes for several years and, within hours, huge queues formed at railway stations. The mass evacuation of British children, the biggest movement of people the country had ever witnessed, had begun.

The next day, September 2, Jean, Ivy and James Thorn – together with countless others – were also evacuated from key towns and cities to the relative safety of the countryside. Many evacuees were with their new parents the next morning when, in stunned silence, they heard Neville Chamberlain inform them that Britain was at war with Germany. What had been sold to the children as

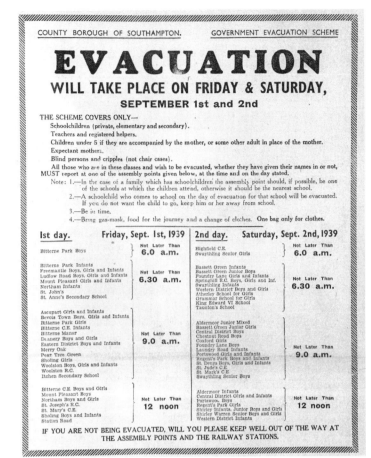

above: **The Southampton evacuation notice which appeared in the Southern Daily Echo detailing assembly points and information about the town's great evacuation on September 1 and 2, 1939.**

a short country holiday now assumed a more permanent reality. The new parents also contemplated the prospect of longer-term disruption to old routines.

The mass evacuations of September 1 and 2 had been a truly formidable planning operation involving around 3.5 million British schoolchildren, mums with toddlers under five, expectant women and the disabled. The advisory note for Southampton parents, which had been issued by the Education Office in April 1939, stated that each child was allowed hand luggage for the trip consisting of "a gas-mask, a change of underclothing, night clothes, house shoes or plimsolls, spare stocking or socks, a toothbrush, knife, fork, spoon, mug and plate, comb, towel and handkerchief". Each traveller was also asked to carry food for the journey. No bottles could be taken and an apple or an orange would "take the place of drinks".

The advisory note stressed that the scheme was voluntary. It further noted: "It will not be possible for mothers to

accompany schoolchildren unless they happen also to be expectant mothers, or unless they also have children under school age whom they wish to be evacuated. The schoolchildren will, however, be accompanied by their teachers and helpers who will remain in the billeting (destination) areas with them, and every effort will be made to continue their schooling. Board and lodging will be provided for the schoolchildren in every case. Lodging will be provided for mothers and children under school age and for other sections, but an allowance for board will only be granted in necessitous cases."

Elementary and secondary schools were used as assembly points for the evacuation and advertisements in the Southern Daily Echo gave full details. So the bewildered children, a mass of cheeky grins and tear-stained faces, clutching bags and cases, gathered for a journey to an unknown destination and a life with strangers.

For some it was a huge adventure. Others were hysterical at the prospect of leaving. An Echo reporter observed: "It was impossible to remain unmoved as childish footsteps echoed along Manor Farm Road this gloomy September morning to herald Southampton's first evacuation assembly. Children of all ages sat in brilliantly-lit classrooms. Some of the toddlers were not properly awake. Others, a bit older, were playing about, blissfully unaware of what was happening."

One of the main concerns was that children would get lost so they were tagged with labels. Their gas-masks were also hung around their necks. They would never forget the feel of the small cardboard box containing the mask bumping against their legs as they struggled with their meagre possessions.

right: Young Southampton evacuees.

The majority of Southampton's children were dispatched to reception areas in Dorset and north Hampshire from where they were "picked" by their new families who were paid 8s (40p) a week by the state to look after each child. In these situations, less attractive children would often be left milling at the end of the queue while adult fingers pointed to their more angelic peers. Mums with babies were not a particularly popular choice either and could also find themselves waiting in a hall as eyes fleetingly settled on them before moving quickly on.

Children's experiences in their new homes – or "billets" – varied enormously. Some foster parents treated evacuated children as well as their own. The health of children transplanted to the country also dramatically improved in some cases. Others were treated like servants, even slaves. Some children were split up from their brothers and sisters, which added to the loneliness and distress, while others found themselves completely alone at night for the first time in their lives.

Bed-wetting became a common problem. Some children were cruelly neglected or even abused. In cases of desperate unhappiness, it was common for parents to come and collect their distraught offspring and take them home. In other cases, parents turned up for their children simply because they missed them and wanted to get the family back together again.

For Jean Thorn, the 11-year-old who made a bid for freedom, the experience of evacuation was traumatic. She recalls:

From the moment I arrived at the house in Christchurch with my sister Ivy, we were made

below: Evacuees from Southampton arrive at Talbot Woods School in Bournemouth with food parcels tied around their necks.

15

to feel unwelcome. The owners' daughter was also staying there with her two children. While they were treated well, we had to eat separately and were told to go to bed early. We also had all the daily chores reserved for us – sweeping snow, digging and painting fences - while the other children just watched. When the house was being cleaned, Ivy and I were also ordered out into the garden even during freezing winter weather. The owners' grandchildren again simply stayed in the warm and watched. We were never loved and were just dogsbodies.

Christchurch itself wasn't much better. We never felt part of the community or even welcome there. People tended to avoid the evacuees as if we had a strange plague. We were completely alienated. We were viewed as an invading army by the local children and treated as such. Our school was housed in a church hall with cloth to divide the rooms while the local children all went to a beautiful school up the road.

My little escape was hilarious when I think about it now but there was a terrible fuss when we were returned to the house by the police. Hundreds of questions were asked and in the end the couple didn't want us any more. My brother James, sister Ivy and I came back home to our house in Victory Road, Millbrook. It was a good job James got home because he was terribly homesick and had come out in bad

rashes as a result. We had been away ten months and once home my mum said: "If we're going to die in the bombing, we can at least all die together from now on."

Ten-year-old Dorothy Fagan was evacuated to Poole in Dorset with her brother and suffered a similar fate.

I was evacuated from Radcliffe Road in Northam, Southampton, with my brother, Donnan. He ended up on one side of a road in Poole with a lot of other boys while I ended up on the other with a very old couple who were extremely house-proud. All the prettiest and nicest children had been picked first and because I wasn't a particularly good-looking child I ended up with these strict pensioners. It was a terrible shock because my mum was very free and easy at home and now I couldn't move for fear of getting into trouble. I had this huge bedroom and on top of a wardrobe at the end of the bed was a huge statue of Jesus with his arms outstretched. That statue used to frighten me to death at night and I used to wet the bed. Then the next day my pyjama trousers were hung around my neck as punishment. There was also a shed at the bottom of the garden with a small gap between it and the fence. It was infested with spiders and I used to be shoved in there as punishment. I actually fainted in there before the owners came and got me.

I spent all my time across the road with my brother and the rest of the kids over there and didn't go to school. Their house was the complete opposite to mine – it was a tip but they were as happy as sandboys in there. They were living like pigs and the couple who owned it just didn't care at all.

I was there two months and then wrote to my mum. I told her I hated it and she came to get me. The old lady told my mum she couldn't take me but there was no stopping her. My mum shoved her out of the way and took me out while the old lady threatened to get the police. Then my mum got my brother and he looked so dirty she didn't want to take him home on the train. My dad came for him in a truck but unlike me he didn't want to leave. He actually cried when he left. We moved around as a family after that but eventually returned to Northam.

For Ronald Lyons, aged nine-and-a-half, evacuation from Chapel Road in Southampton to Swanage in Dorset was a positive experience. He recalls:

I remember a special song was being played on the radio to help us youngsters settle in. It was called "Goodnight Children Everywhere". The song went: "Goodnight children everywhere; your mother's with you night and day; put your head upon your pillow; don't be a kid or a weeping willow; close your eyes and say a prayer; maybe you'll find a kiss to spare; though she's far away, she's with you night and day; goodnight children everywhere." I went down to Dorset with one of my brothers, Terrence. I was tearful when I went but I was treated fine and settled in with a policeman's family in their town centre house. I remember the smell of the lovely clean sheets and pillows more than anything else which was a change from the poverty we were enduring in Southampton. My brother didn't stay in the same place – he ended up staying with a millionaire in his mansion overlooking Swanage which was like visiting another planet for him. Then my mum eventually came down with the other nine children and we all lived as a family in Swanage. My dad worked in the Southampton Docks and used to come down at weekends. He used to cycle the whole way.

On another occasion my mother went to see Dad in Southampton and two of my brothers, five-year-old Reggie and six-year-old Leonard, waited at Swanage Station for her return. Someone then came

"WE HAD AN ESCAPED GERMAN PRISONER HIDING IN OUR HOUSE LAST NIGHT!"
"HOW DID YOU KNOW?"
"I HEARD MUM TELL DAD THERE WAS A JERRY UNDER THE BED!"

up to them and told them the train with Mum on had been blown up by a bomb. They burst into tears on the platform but it transpired that Mum had missed that train because she was delayed. The boys were all smiles again when she eventually came back to Swanage.

Eleven-year-old Pat Malone left Radcliffe Road for Dorset and also had a happy experience. He recalls:

I went to stay with my aunt in Sturminster Newton. It was a lovely cottage and so, so different from the terraced streets of Southampton. The thing I remember was the freedom and amazing space. We just roamed the fields and explored. It was like travelling to another world. I was taught to sing hymns and dig allotments and not a lot else apart from playing and making catapults. We went to the village school but it was very different from Northam Boys' School in Southampton. There was a lady teacher for a start and it was a lot easier going. No-one walked around with a cane behind their back which made a nice change. We were in the great outdoors most of the time and it was fantastic just roaming the fields. The smells were different, so were the animals, it was just great being there. I became a proper Dorset boy and even acquired the accent in the end and so did lots of others. Only the Cockney Londoners seemed to keep their accents.

I used to stay at the same cottage during our

normal school holidays so during the evacuation it just seemed like one great long, continuous adventure.

Then there is this idyllic report which appeared in the Southern Daily Echo at the time. A group of "thirty little Sotonians" evacuated to Marshwood in Beaminster, Dorset, submitted a letter which read:

left: **Pat Malone who was evacuated to this cottage in Sturminster Newton.**

"For the first few weeks, nine of us were billeted in a parish hall at Bettiscombe, but now we are nearly all living on farms, where we are learning many things which we could not see and learn in the town. At first we found the Dorset speech very funny and we find this a windy district. In the summer we had plenty of apples. Picking them was great fun … in the summer holiday we went blackberrying and between us picked 150 pounds which we sold at 3d (1p) a pound in Bridport Market. With the money we bought wool which we knitted into articles for the Forces and Save the Children Fund."

The letter continued: "Many of us have learned to milk cows, and some of us milk two or three regularly each day. We used to get up at 5.30am. Many of us have learned how to pluck fowls and prepare them for market, and we help the farmers regularly by feeding the poultry."

Teacher Reg Ward and wife Muriel, a school helper, escorted a large party of children from Merry Oak School in Bitterne to Poole. He recalls:

For the first two weeks, we busied ourselves visiting all the homes used by our children and kept in touch with the "Aunties" who looked after them. The children soon started at schools in Poole and the Mayor of Southampton came down to visit them in early 1940. Some of our children returned home in the first couple of months due to homesickness and sometimes we would have to set off on a jaunt to find a new billet if a child was unhappy. But every Monday evening we held "socials" at Emerson Hall in Parkstone, Poole, which cheered everyone up. There was table tennis, card games, bagatelle, community games, country dancing and competitions. Children also made models, did sketches, knitted and took part in one-act plays usually of a blood and thunder variety!

The Poole teachers were always so willing to help the Southampton children and the youngsters were generally very happy. I remember one young lad from a very poor background who was taken in by a 75-year-old lady. That old lady became more precious to him than his own parents. The boy's parents took him home in the end and it was a very tearful parting.

I also remember fetching another girl from hospital where she had undergone a slight operation. I carried her from the car to the house and the whole host family was waiting for her. A special fire had been lit in the best room and toys, some of which had been bought for the occasion, awaited her.

On the other hand, while most Southampton parents were naturally concerned about their children, others seemed to disclaim responsibility for them. Some of these children had no letters or messages from home. We were also astonished at some of the cases of uncleanliness, bad habits and bad language. Some of these children were used to sleeping in their day clothes.

Meanwhile, the boys from King Edward's Grammar School in Southampton joined up with the girls from Poole's Parkstone Grammar and formed an Evacuees' Club. They staged plays, did voluntary work, tended an allotment and some became teachers in the Sunday School. Overall, the people of Poole were magnificent and made us feel very welcome indeed.

While the evacuees settled in, Hitler's

invasion of Poland sent a severe jolt reverberating through the communities they left behind. Britain had been shaken out of its appeasement malaise overnight. Many now expected massed air fleets of bombers to arrive overhead bringing death on a cataclysmic scale. There would surely be gas attacks. Mustard gas would descend, perhaps even the deadlier Lewisite gas.

Southampton, with its port complex, the Thornycroft shipbuilding yard and the Supermarine Spitfire factory would surely be a major target. Alarmist estimates began to circulate: each ton of explosive would result in fifty casualties at least. Southampton's citizens literally looked up at the sky from their doorsteps as if expecting a dark swarm of enemy bombers to appear that instant. They looked along the road to discover their neighbours doing exactly the same, searching for hell in the heavens.

Preparation for terror dramatically moved up a gear. Strange indicator boards popped up all over the town. They were painted with a special substance which would change colour if gas was poisoning the atmosphere. Sandbags – some half-a-million of them – appeared everywhere too and they were piled beneath the Bargate arch to prepare it as a shelter. Static water tanks materialised in readiness for fire and filled buckets were placed in gardens to await the firestorms.

Families also fumbled with government-issued gas-masks, officially described as "civilian-type respirators", which they were urged to carry with them at all times. Everyone had a gas-mask and it was the first time the British public had entered a war armed with an item of self-defence. They were hot and sweaty to wear and initially difficult to put on. First the chin was placed inside the rubber and then the mask pulled over the face. Besides the standard adult model, special Mickey Mouse designs were available for infants between two and two-and-a-half. They were painted red and blue and had large floppy ears but were later withdrawn due to scarce resources.

Babies under the age of two were encased in a special gas helmet similar to a miniature iron lung. Once inside,

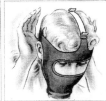

parents used bellows to pump air into the strange dome. There was also a cradle covered by a Perspex lid which could be used to cocoon a baby for the same purpose. Parents had to think up elaborate games to encourage children to get used to the strange, new devices.

Older children naturally delighted in donning their masks and leaping out to terrify younger siblings. Women meanwhile found that the cardboard gas-mask box could double up as a handbag and covers were even sold to make them more attractive. For men, glamour models on posters and postcards encouraged gas-mask usage. One, featuring a model clutching a mask, cheekily proclaimed: "I'm ready for anything!" Gas-masks soon assumed a range of nicknames with

above: **Gas attack advice poster.**

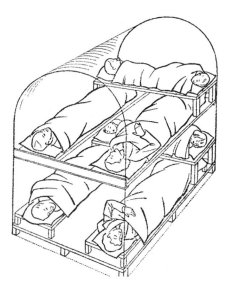

above: **Anderson advice leaflet: how to sleep four adults and four babies inside a shelter.**

above: **Gas-mask for Mum and helmet for baby into which small bellows pumped air.**

"nosebags" the preferred adult choice while children called theirs a "Hitler". Woolworth's in Above Bar, Southampton, also sold sixpenny (2.5p) tin hats for children which were very popular. They were effectively useless but the youngsters felt reassured wearing them.

As Southampton awaited the bombers, Anderson shelters were issued and hastily dug into gardens. The shelters, named after Sir John Anderson, the Home Secretary at the beginning of the war, were cheap and easy to construct and consisted of several curved sections of corrugated steel bolted together at the top and sunk 3 feet (91 cms) into the ground.

It was recommended that at least 15 inches (38 cms) of soil be piled on top and shelters came with the guarantee that they would protect up to six adults against anything bar a direct hit. Sandbags were stacked against the rear and front walls of the tunnel shelter. Some residents planted them as rock gardens and even vegetables were grown on them too. Solid entrance doors were prohibited since they would prevent fresh air circulating. A blanket was simply draped from a curtain rail instead. Many of these shelters were dug the day after war was declared and there were frantic scenes as fathers grabbed spades and stormed out into the garden. Drainage problems followed and baling out was a constant headache.

Nonetheless, by September 1939, nearly one-and-a-half-million shelters had been distributed free to British families with incomes of less than £250 a year. Families practised their shelter drills, packed vital papers and made their garden homes as comfortable as possible. Beds measuring 2 feet in width (61cm) and made from timber frames, wire netting and stretched canvas were recommended as was bedding consisting of army blankets converted into sleeping bags and stuffed with pockets of newspaper. Layers of newspaper also

below: **Workers wearing gas-masks preparing for the worst at the Southampton British American Tobacco factory.**

provided the mattress. Shelters were cold and damp and full of slugs, beetles and earwigs. Cramped conditions brought their own hygiene problems and an advice pamphlet suggested snorers put a cotton reel in the middle of their backs to prevent them from lying in a position which exacerbated the problem. Hot water bottles or hot house bricks wrapped in an old vest meanwhile provided individual warmth.

For those without gardens, there was the Morrison shelter – a strong steel table with mesh sides for use inside the house. Public shelters were also opened around the town. During the month before the war began, 100 basement shelters – for the most part medieval wine cellars – were opened in the older parts of Southampton to provide accommodation for 10,000. The central archway of the Bargate was also bricked up to make a street shelter and a large letter "S" painted on the pavement indicated the location of other public shelters in the town. Provision of both Anderson and public shelters was exceptionally good in Southampton. More than 30,000 Andersons were distributed and public shelters could house a further 25,000.

Then it went dark. Southampton became a town of the night and one capable of arousing the most primitive fears during the "blackout". The first blackout exercise to be staged in England was carried out in Southampton in 1937. Now it was the real thing and no light could be emitted for fear of helping bombers find their target. Brown sticky paper was pasted in windows and black cloth curtain draped across as well. Homes became unbearably hot and stuffy in summer and often remained dark all day in winter.

Outside, a simple walk could become a perilous expedition, a family outing a major operation. Citizens would actually walk into lamp-posts or each other. They literally groped about and adopted what some contributors jokingly recall as the "Blackout Walk" with arms outstretched before them. Traffic accidents increased and petty criminals took full advantage.

One attempted solution, though it never worked, was to wear illuminated badges or, for the fashion-conscious, 6d (2.5p) "glow in the dark" flowers pinned to coats. In fact the estimated amount of light which could be seen by an enemy bomber was hopelessly overestimated. It was even reported in London that a man

AIR RAID PRECAUTIONS

PROVISION OF PROTECTION FOR PERSONS CAUGHT IN THE STREETS ON THE RECEIPT OF THE AIR RAID WARNING

THE TRENCHES SCHEDULED BELOW:

TRENCH	LOCALITY	Number of Persons Accommodated
East Park	Adjoining East Park Terrace; New Road (Approach)	— 135
Vincent's Walk	Above Bar Street, Pound Tree Road (Approach)	— 150
Sussex Place	West Side, Kingsland Place, adjoining Sussex Road	— 150
Hoglands	Houndwell Road and lower part of St. Mary's Place	— 280
Hill Lane	Southampton Common, West Side, opposite Bellemoor Rd.	270
Millbrook Rec.	Millbrook Road, 500 feet west of Regents Park Road	— 390
Shirley Rec.	Winchester Road, junction St. James Road	— 270
Pear Tree Green	Pear Tree Green, lower part of Peartree Avenue	— 110
Veracity Ground	Junction Shaling Road, Spring Road; Woolston	— 110
Archery Ground	Junction Archery Road, Swift Road; Woolston	— 122
Inner Avenue	The Avenue, opposite Middle Street	— 200
Northam Rec.	Summer Street, off Northam Road, just below Northam Bridge	— 160
Bitterne Rec.	West End Road; 500 feet from junction Bitterne Road, West End Road	— 150

Directional Signs are placed on lamp and tramway columns and marked "PUBLIC SHELTER" in black letters on white ground, and arrows in white paint on kerbs to indicate the nearest route to the Shelter.

Each Shelter (trench) is marked by a sign on which is shown the number of persons the trench will accommodate.

THE UNDERMENTIONED BASEMENT SHELTERS SCHEDULED BELOW ARE BEING ADAPTED AND AS THEY BECOME AVAILABLE FOR USE NOTIFICATION WILL BE GIVEN.

ADDRESS	Number of Persons
"Red Lion" Hotel, Sea Road, Woolston	78
"Drummond" Hotel, Radstock Road, Woolston	60
Messrs. Lankester & Son, West Street	96
Messrs. Edwin Jones & Co., Ltd., Warehouse, Town Quay	158
Union Bank Chambers, Holy Rood	178
Messrs. Phippards, 22-23 High Street	177
Messrs. Gillet's Meat Market, South Front	120
Old Lloyds Bank, High Street	70
Messrs. Cox & Sharland, High Street	60
Century Wine Stores, 6 Bernard Street	40
British Thompson Houston, 6 West Street	60
8, 10 and 11 St. Michael Square	344
Messrs. Simper & Co., Back-of-the-Walls	144
Elders & Fyffes Ltd., 80a High Street	188
Gaiety Picture House, High Street	110
Rev. H. G. Goodall, 28 Bugle Street	106
Messrs. Toogood's Seed Warehouse, Millbrook	1580
Bargate Hotel	138
Van Allan, Ltd., 151, Above Bar	84
Messrs. Baines & Owen, 5, High Street	75
Messrs. Hollis, The Strand	143
Shops, Addis Square, Portswood Road	595
Messrs. Toogoods' Shop, 45, London Road	200
St. Barnabas' Church and Vestry, Lodge Road	117
Royal Insurance Co., Ltd., 67, Above Bar	116
Messrs. Scrases' Brewery, Back of the Walls	1257
Whole of Portland Street	261
Messrs. Goodwin, Back of the Walls	100
Under Town Walls, Western Esplanade	200
St. John's School, French Street	60
Undercroft, Simnel Street	120
Central Bridge, 3, Arches	390
Central Bridge, 6, Arches	800
Audit House, High Street	450
J. Frisby, Ltd., 201, Portswood Road	75
International Tea Co.'s Stores, Ltd., 199, Portswood Road	75

The positions of Basement Shelters are shown by signboards painted white with "PUBLIC SHELTER" and number of persons that can be accommodated painted in black lettering.

The Public are requested in the event of an Air Raid to proceed quietly to the nearest Shelter, taking respirators, and to remain seated and keep still until raid is over.

left: The list detailing where the town's public shelters and trenches were located and how many could be accommodated in them.

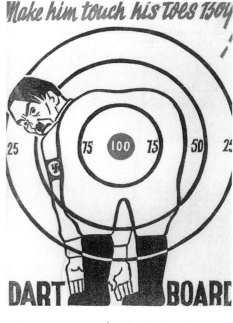

right: Children's novelty Hitler dartboard.

Make him touch his toes 1504

DART BOARD

below: The Black-Out! card game.

was stopped from puffing too hard on his cigar for fear it could be seen by the enemy.

While the preparations were stepped up, a range of government booklets and pamphlets was produced to stem rising panic and settle the populous. One, entitled "What is to be done if a crisis occurs?", advised reading the Southern Daily Echo for details and preparing luggage, gas-masks and food ready for travel; another was called "Can You Tell Me? A Blitz Quiz of 50 Types of Question and Their Answers". It included information on burial arrangements, adopting orphaned children and how to trace a missing family. Books also appeared advising how to spot enemy aircraft. The "ABC of Aeroplane Spotting" included handy silhouette sketches, which compared the shape of British and German warplanes.

There was no shortage of advice to parents on how to keep youngsters amused during the monotonous hours likely to be spent in shelters and blacked-out homes. "Try games," suggested the Southern Daily Echo. "The most interesting game is Throwing The Smile. You all sit in a very solemn circle except the first player who wears a broad grin. Then he puts his hand to his face and pretends to wipe off the smile and throw it to another player. The second player smiles in turn, wipes off the smile and throws it to someone else and so on. No-one must smile except the two players concerned and anyone who does so out of turn is out of the game. The one who never loses his gravity is the winner."

Sing-songs were also "highly recommended" and the game of Lexicon was promoted as providing "hours of fun and entertainment during the black-out nights". There was also the "amusing, topical card game, Black-Out – the game to cheer you up!"

Toys also began to adopt a war theme and were designed to bring fun to gloomy homes and shelters. They

right: **Boo-Boo's bravery against the enemy made him a hit with young readers.**

below right: **Barrage balloons over Southampton Docks.**

below: **Comic postcards with a cheeky theme.**

included dartboards featuring an open-mouthed Hitler at the bulls-eye and battle jigsaws. There was also the inspired Decorate Goering, the New Party Game. It took the concept of Pinning the Tail on the Donkey and instead invited children to close their eyes and stick a medal belonging to the German Air Chief on his body. It invariably ended up in a variety of interesting and hilarious places.

Adults took to reading to wind away the hours. Demand for books soared and libraries noticed a surge in interest in current affairs, texts on modern Germany and, above all, Hitler's Mein Kampf (My Struggle).

Publisher's Longmans even published an anthology called The Shelter Book to "keep shelterers company in the life of huddle, hard bunks … improvised sanitation, vacuum flasks, torches and community singing". The Black-Out Book was published in 1939 and featured George Bernard Shaw and other famous personalities as well as amusing "schoolboy howlers" and "juvenile wit".

High above Southampton's shelters, barrage balloons appeared. These huge lumbering inflatables were a passive form of defence and designed to force enemy raiders to fly higher and so hinder bombing accuracy. They were tethered by wires which would slice like giant axes if an aircraft hit them. These balloons began to feature in children's literature. Blossom the Brave Balloon held Hitler's air force at bay while Boo Boo, with his elephantine features, once sent a bomber crashing to earth. "Then," concluded the tale, "Boo Boo was indeed proud and happy that he had done his duty and helped save the land he loved."

In the adult world, scarcity, shortage and queuing became a way of life. Food rationing had begun in January 1940 during one of the coldest winters on record. Most food, especially fruit and meat, was imported from overseas and wartime disruption to world trade made Britain vulnerable to chronic shortages, even starvation. Within a week of war being declared, a separate government body was inaugurated, The Ministry of Food, under Lord Woolton. The market alone could not be allowed to remedy the

problem by simply reflecting shortages in higher prices. Millions of working class people would then have gone without while the richer tiers of society purchased the scant stocks available.

It quickly became apparent that rationing of foods and essential goods would have to be enforced instead. Most foods were rationed either by their weight, a special points rating or cost. Hence, essential foods for each person were rationed at 1s 10d (9p) worth of meat per week, three pints of milk, eight ounces of sugar, four ounces of butter or fat, four ounces of bacon, two ounces

of tea, one ounce of cheese and one egg. Other foods such as rice, jam, biscuits, tinned food and dried fruit were rationed by points and coupons were used to buy them. If there was an excess of any particular product, the points required to purchase would be lowered so that more could be bought for each coupon. The reverse strategy was implemented if there was a sudden shortage of a particular item.

Fish was never rationed. In fact it was virtually impossible to obtain any during the war and the British became introduced to tuna, snook and whale meat for the first time. There were no problems with bread, however. It was in constant supply even though millers ground more of the husks into the flour to make it go further when wheat and flour were in short supply. The Ministry

of Food actually prohibited white bread, stating that it did not contain enough vitamins and so paved the way for brown bread, the Hovis loaf and husk bread.

Substitute food also made its first appearance. Many households used saccharine tablets as an alternative to sugar, margarine instead of butter and milk powder, potato powder and egg powder which was popular in Yorkshire puddings, scrambled eggs and omelettes. Then there were the new foods. Spam was introduced from America and could be eaten hot or cold; corned beef arrived from New Zealand and Argentina and was cheap, fatty and strong tasting; pilchards appeared in grocery shops where previously fresh herring had been available from fishmongers and salmon arrived from Canada for those with money to spend.

above: **Before the bombers came: Above Bar, Southampton, in the 1930s.**

Rationing did not affect offal – such as hearts, liver and kidneys – and large bones that still had amounts of meat on them were heavily in demand. A variety of new dishes also originated such as tripe and onions, faggots and Pease pudding. Tea, meanwhile, was not rationed until July 1940 and sweets followed two years later when an allocation of points restricted consumption to three ounces per head per week.

Each family had to register with a shop or store where foodstuffs would be bought and this was to be the only place where such purchases could be made. In addition, each family member had his or her own ration book – buff coloured for adults, blue for children over three, and green for babies – so that purchasing could be monitored and recorded. Children were subtly encouraged to conserve, too. They could buy their own miniature scales to "help weigh your mummy's meat ration" while a Dolly Ration Book could be used to carefully measure and record a favourite doll's food intake.

Ironically, the health of many people improved following food rationing as the nation's citizens tucked into new delights like turnip pie and haricot beans. Further, there had never been such awareness of the need for a balanced diet and a huge range of cookbooks and pamphlets containing nutritious recipes appeared. Again, children were not excluded and booklets like Potato Pete's Nursery Rhymes encouraged vegetable consumption and healthy eating.

The rationing of clothing followed food in June 1941. The allowance was forty-eight coupons per year per person and it applied to everyone. All clothes items in the shops thereafter had a price tag plus the number of coupons required to purchase them. An individual's buying power was therefore determined by the number of allocated coupons rather than how much money they had. The whole system was not designed to affect price. It was merely to restrict supply. Hence, a shirt or blouse could cost 2s 6d (12.5p) plus three coupons and the item could be purchased only if the shopper had

right: **Making new clothes from old.** This advertisement advised: "Schoolgirls love pinafore dresses. This illustration shows a neat up-to-date design which can be made from a flared edge-to-edge coat with a panel back."

below: "Fur trimmed and very smart." This advertisement suggests: "Perhaps you have the coat of a tunic suit in good condition, but the skirt well worn. Since the tunic coat is now quite out of date why not make it into a coat for a schoolgirl?"

left: The advertisement reads: "A man's overcoat which is not too heavy in weight can be made into a smart coat for his small son."

the cash and the required coupons. The clothing coupons were also transferable. If a household wished to buy a girl's dress costing six coupons, three could come from the wife's allowance and three from her husband's.

The forty-eight clothes coupons a year did not go very far. A raincoat would require seven coupons, a man's suit eight, trousers six, a man's shirt four, a girl's gym kit four, shoes and boots two, and a lady's dress five. Improvisation and conservation was therefore the key to sensible household management. Old

jumpers were picked to make new garments; the "tails" of men's shirts could make a small boy's top; and the bottom legs of adult trousers could make a small child's pair. Children, meanwhile, had to be educated in how to look after their clothes and the government slogan "Make do and Mend" appeared everywhere and reverberated around households.

One material in particular was in great demand during this period of acute scarcity. Disused parachutes – made from the finest parachute silk – were snapped up and turned into silk dresses, "best"

shirts, blouses, ties and handkerchiefs. New products also came on the market to assist such as Rynchene which saved clothing coupons by "making old garments look and feel like new".

Three weeks after the outbreak of war, petrol rationing was introduced. The car was mainly a luxury which only the middle and upper classes could afford but, once again, cash and the correct number of coupons were required for petrol purchase. Pleasure motoring was banned – a move which caused an outcry among the privileged and in the seaside towns which enjoyed their custom.

Each car was allowed between four and ten gallons of petrol per month at 1s 6d (7p) per gallon. The flexible allocation reflected differing sizes of car. It was estimated that this arrangement would enable motorists to cover an average of seven miles a day and up to 200 miles per month if they drove carefully. Siphoning and petrol theft became common and private garages were used to hoard personal supplies of petrol. Cars were not frequently used, however, due to the blackout. Indeed, motoring, with headlamp beams restricted to narrow strips, proved to be highly dangerous.

Public transport also had its problems. Fuel supplies were being absorbed by the armed forces and buses were taken out of service by 9pm during the week and 2pm on Sundays. Buses did not run at all on Sundays in some provincial towns. Rail travel did not have a coupon-style restriction imposed upon it but another mode of transport became increasingly preferred: the bicycle. Sales soared and the bike proved to be the quickest way to travel once roads became blocked or littered with debris from air raids.

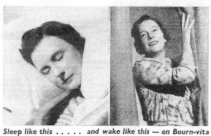

The salary scale and the cost of living must finally be considered to complete a picture of pre-Blitz Southampton. All men and women had to register for work and most were engaged in the armed services. Others were employed in home defence duties such as the Home Guard or Air Raid Precautions Services (ARP) and perhaps 60,000 were conscientious objectors of whom 5,000 were sent to prison.

The outbreak of war actually led to a period of prosperity for many sections of the population because extra work suddenly became available for both men and women. Servicemen's families were the worst off but many households derived income from a husband, wife and children employed in occupations serving the war effort. Working class employees in particular saw a substantial rise in their incomes when they switched from their peacetime employment to "war jobs" in aircraft or armament

factories. The average man's wage in fact rose from a pre-war sum of £2 17s 6d (£2.87p) to around £4 a week while a woman's salary increased from 35s a week (£1.75p) to £2 15s (£2.75).

However, the weekly household expenses of a working class family of five, as suggested by the Daily Express in 1940, amounted to a total of £3 when such items as rent, coal, gas, electricity and clothes were included. The difficulty of household management is further highlighted when the cost of basic foodstuffs is considered. Butter, for example, was priced at 1s 6d (7p) per pound; Cheddar cheese at 10d (4p) per pound; Danish side bacon at 1s 6d (7p) per pound; milk at 3d (1p) per pint; Player's cigarettes at 7d (3p) for ten; and St Bruno tobacco at 1s 2d (6p) per ounce. These prices inevitably rose with shortages, squeezing budgets still further.

As far as treats were concerned, cinema and theatre tickets could cost

above:
Southampton's bustling town centre in the 1930s. The old Southern Daily Echo offices can be seen to the left. The Palace Theatre is a short distance up the street.

Did you **MACLEAN** your teeth to-day?

Aye, Aye, both fore and aft

Obtainable everywhere 6ᴰ, 10½ᴰ & 1/6 **MACLEANS** PEROXIDE **TOOTH PASTE**

Macleans patented pure white nozzle keeps the toothpaste fresh and clean from first squeeze to last.

BRITISH TO THE TEETH

1-2s (5-10p) while, at the other end of the scale, a live-in maid would require a salary of £1 per week. For those considering extra mobility, a new standard Vauxhall car cost £159 while a top 80 m.p.h. De Luxe Saloon model boasting "extremely luxurious finish and appointments" required £330 for purchase.

Unsurprisingly, rising costs coupled with rationing made life extremely tough for many such as the Lyons family in Southampton. Patrick and Kitty Lyons had eleven children in their terraced house in Chapel Road. Their nine-and-a-half-year-old son, Ronald, the boy who was evacuated to Swanage with brother Terrence, recalls:

Our family was basically poverty-stricken. At five I didn't understand why we kept moving from house to house but I eventually realised it was because we couldn't afford the rent. We had no sheets or blankets and only had army coats thrown over us for warmth. We also relied heavily on the Red Cross for clothes and shoes. We kids called an Oxo cube

our one square meal of the day. We were always hungry and every degrading thing happened. We were not alone of course. The Chapel area in those days was like a slum, a ghetto. There was a family near us with twenty-two children living in the same terrible conditions. There was no heating in these places either. We simply wheeled an old pram down to Northam and looked for any bits of coke which we could take back for the fire. As for the toilet, that was just a hole in the ground in a hut at the end of the garden. I remember feeling absolutely shattered all the time because there was no breakfast and we were trying to sleep in the shelters all the time. So school suffered. I could never concentrate due to the cold, hunger and tiredness and we were told to rest our heads on our arms when we got to school to make up for the lost sleep. I also remember standing at the gates of my school, St Joseph's in St Michael's Square. My mum would give my older brother some pennies to buy buns from the baker and he would bring them down to the school and pass them through the railings.

A black market rapidly developed to cater for needs with goods originating from docks and bond stores. Some shopkeepers kept goods "under the counter" for their poorer regulars and also "marked up" prices to deter occasional visitors. Yet while belts were tightened and preparations continued, there was still no sign of the bombers. Southampton was ready and waiting but the skies were strangely clear. What had been experienced was a curious lull that came to be known as the "Bore War" or "Twilight War" and then by the Americanism, the "Phoney War".

As the raids failed to materialise, many parents set off to collect their evacuated children and brought them home in time for the Christmas of 1939. By January 1940, it was estimated that two-fifths of the nation's children had returned home and between 400,000 and one million were receiving little or no education. Yet, despite the perceived lull, the global chess game was changing and key moves were about to be made.

On May 10, 1940, Winston Churchill succeeded Chamberlain as Prime Minister. Seventeen days later, an armada of vessels began to evacuate 338,000 trapped Allied troops from the beaches of Dunkirk in France while approaching German Panzer

tanks inexplicably stopped in their tracks. Hitler had ordered them to stop on May 24 in order to allow infantry support to catch up and bring in the Luftwaffe. It was a strategically inept decision and one which gave the stranded Allied troops a vital chance to escape. During the nights of June 2 and 3, the remainder of the British units and 60,000 French troops were brought out. However 30,000 had been wounded, captured or killed on the sands.

Britain was on her knees. Herbert Morrison, then Minister of Supply, voiced one of the great rallying cries of the war – "Go To It" – as he urged the country's workers to put every last ounce of energy into the struggle. However the country was exhausted, demoralised – and now alone against Hitler.

The British troops who had left Southampton for France now returned to the port after the disaster at Dunkirk. It was a desperately sad sight. Local children watched along Weston Shore as train wagons painted with huge red crosses brought the limp, bandaged and bewildered remnants of the army into the town. A huge camp was set up at the Veracity Ground and homes in

Merry Oak Road opened their doors and invited the filthy troops to have a bath. Many French soldiers stayed at Bitterne Park School in Manor Farm Road where residents squeezed cakes and sandwiches through the railings. For several nights, some 2,000 French soldiers also used the Guildhall as army quarters.

During the Dunkirk calamity, the British Expeditionary Force had left nearly 2,500 guns, some 400 tanks and more than 60,000 other vehicles behind in France. The RAF had also lost 509 fighters in the war already. Of fifty British destroyers taking part in the evacuation, nine had been sunk and twenty-three damaged.

Britain expected an immediate invasion – and there seemed little she could do to repel it. Then, on June 10, Italy also declared war on both Britain and France.

On June 18, 1940, Churchill rose to his feet in the House of Commons and said: "…The Battle of France is over. I expect that the Battle of Britain is about to begin…the whole fury and might of the enemy must very soon be turned on us. Hitler knows that he will have to break us in this island or lose the war... Let us therefore brace ourselves to our duties, and so bear ourselves that, if the British Empire and its Commonwealth last for a thousand years, men will still say, 'This was their finest hour.'"

Within twenty-four hours, German Air Chief Hermann Goering had taken the wraps off a pet project – the "Luftschlacht um England", his air attack on England. It was a perfect June night in Southampton when he sent the first wave of bombers to the South Coast. Many of the town's inhabitants had spent the evening in their gardens, some industriously, others lounging in deck chairs. Some were still chatting across garden gates when the sirens began their strange up and down wailing. Then came a faint, ominous hum from the heavens. Next a drone – a monotonous, mechanical dirge – filled the sky.

It was 11.17 pm on June 19, 1940. The talk was over. It really was going to happen after all. Fathers shouted orders. Mothers gathered broods. The elderly and infirm joined the hurried human procession to shelters.

Now the wait. Then, far, far above, the black cloak of night tipped out its deadly contents. Ten high explosive bombs were sent hurtling earthbound towards Millbrook. Still silence. Now the deafening, indescribable blasts.

The shattering of glass. The crashing of masonry, the cries and whimpering amid contorted wreckage.

Two high explosive bombs had fallen in South Mill Road, one in Westbury Road, one at the Tobacco Factory entrance and three in Millbrook Road. A huge blaze broke out in Millbrook Road where the White House Garage had received a direct hit. Two hundred houses were already damaged, three obliterated and massive craters transformed Regent's Park Road into a lunar landscape. Dense smoke also enveloped Redbridge when a store containing railway sleepers was hit. Fires blazed at Marchwood and Dibden's little hilltop church was hit too.

More screaming. Panic. Bedlam. One person died from shock. ARP (Air Raid Precautions) men were quickly on the scene and within twenty-five minutes ten injured citizens were safely in hospital. Most of the injured were those who had let curiosity overrule common sense and had stayed out to watch the spectacle.

Gwen Hughes was cowering inside the Anderson shelter at the bottom of her garden in Westbury Road, Southampton, when that first raid began. She recalls:

I was in the shelter with my two children, Anthony, two, and Gloria, five. My husband Monty had frantically dug the shelter in our garden the day after war was declared and had told us to get out

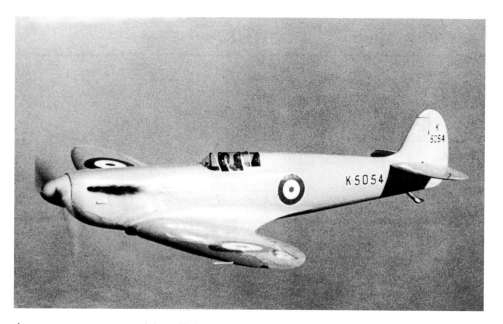

left: The first air-to-air photograph of the prototype Spitfire K5054 taken during the afternoon of May 11, 1936 with Test Pilot Mutt Summers, who undertook the inaugural flight, at the controls. The Spitfire had been perfected just in time. Its inaugural flight on 5 March 1936 occurred just two days before Hitler's troops marched into the Rhineland and world war loomed as an increasing possibility.

there as soon as any siren sounded. An elderly woman from next door was in the shelter too and she was in a terrible state. She kept saying: "Oh my God, Oh my God" and I thought she would frighten my children. I tried to comfort her and the lady's head ended up in my lap. She was terrified but thankfully my children were asleep during the raid. I remember coming out and seeing the terrific damage. The old lady went crazy when she saw what had happened. I thought we had lost our house at first and then realised the two opposite had gone. My dad owned the Melbourne Restaurant in Southampton High Street and he asked me to bring the children down to the shelter there afterwards.

A far more terrifying experience lay in wait for the Hughes family at The Melbourne — however that was five months away. On the morning of June 20, 1940, at five past three to be precise, the all-clear siren sounded after that first night of bombing. Miraculously, there had been just the one fatality.

"The morale of the population was excellent in this, their first experience of air raids," said the Air Raid Precautions report the next day.

The town was buzzing. Crowds came to inspect the damage. They wanted to talk to witnesses. What had it been like? What did it sound like? They would soon find out.

The "Phoney War", the "Bore War", the agonising wait, was over. Sirens would now sound on an almost daily basis. The length of the raids would soon surprise everyone and cramped, damp, poorly ventilated shelters would reek of dirty humanity.

A second mass evacuation of children had started at the end of June and this time whole schools were moved to rural areas. The practice of "trekking" also began. Each evening, large numbers of citizens would leave the town by foot, bicycle or even as part of organised coach parties and head for the relative safety of the countryside where they slept under

left: Spitfire designer Reginald Mitchell. In the 21 years he was at Supermarine, Mitchell designed 24 types of aircraft. His Spitfire prototype K5054 (above) was to be the only Spitfire he saw fly. He died on June 11, 1937, aged just 42.

hedges, in barns and in outhouses before returning the next morning.

The world conflict was now hurtling headlong into a new, deadlier phase. The engine of the German war machine was stoking up, its appetite increasingly voracious and unsatisfied. On July 10, a formation of seventy German Luftwaffe aircraft swarmed towards Britain for aerial combat in the cloudy skies. The German Air Force lost thirteen aircraft to the RAF's six in a confrontation which RAF supremo, Air Chief Marshall Hugh Dowding, would later define as the opening of the "Battle of Britain".

Two days later the bombers returned to Southampton. Four bombs fell out of the sky without warning in the middle of the day and landed in School Road, Hamble – moments after the children had left for the shelters. No-one was hurt.

Then, on July 16, Adolf Hitler issued Directive No. 16 to his inner circle declaring Britain would be invaded "if necessary". "Operation Sea Lion" was at last announced and German Army High Command ordered thirteen handpicked divisions to prepare for the first invasion wave. However, it did not take the Fuehrer and his generals long to realise that invasion would involve a major military operation and substantial risk. It depended effectively on whether the Luftwaffe and the Navy could prepare the way for the landing of German troops in southern England in the face of a far superior British Navy and a far from negligible RAF. If the skies and seas could be cleared, six infantry divisions would leave the Pas de Calais and hit the beaches between Ramsgate and Bexhill; four would cross from Le Havre and land between Brighton and the Isle of Wight; and further west three divisions would leave the Cherbourg peninsula and storm ashore at Lyme Bay. Altogether 90,000 men would form the first wave and by day three it was hoped to get 260,000 troops across to Britain.

The stage was set. Victory in the air would unlock the front door of Britain to the Nazis. There was only one way to get the key: destruction of the Royal Air Force. The gladiators of the sky were thus arranged. On the German side there were

three principle bombers – the Dornier Do 17, nicknamed the "flying pencil" due to its shape, the Heinkel He 111 and the versatile Junkers Ju 88. They would be accompanied by two supporting fighters – the Messerschmitt Bf 109 (an excellent aircraft though fuel supply limited its fighting time over Britain to just ten minutes) and the slower but formidably armed two-engined Messerschmitt Bf 110.

The RAF meanwhile boasted an elegant aircraft which had been designed and was now being manufactured in the Supermarine factory in Woolston, Southampton. Reginald Mitchell had designed a fighter measuring just 36 feet long (11m) by 30 feet wide (9m) and it was called the Spitfire. During the afternoon of Thursday, March 5, 1936, the pristine Spitfire prototype – registration K5054 - had completed its maiden flight above Eastleigh Airport and Mitchell, stricken with cancer and with only fifteen months to live, was there to witness his creation in action. He died knowing it performed up to his expectations and that the government had ordered 310 of them. He would never know, however, that he had effectively handed Britain's young pilots the means with which to prevent invasion. Mitchell's Spitfire was joined in the air by the Hawker Hurricane which made up two thirds of the defending force.

The forces engaged were relatively

above: **Picture taken just hours after Spitfire K5054's maiden flight over Eastleigh showing key members of the team. From left to right: Vickers-Supermarine Chief Test Pilot Capt J "Mutt" Summers, OBE; Major H J Payn, Technical Assistant to R.J. Mitchell; "R J" himself as he was known to all at Supermarine; Stuart Scott-Hall, resident Technical Officer at Supermarine; and lastly Flt Lt Jeffrey Quill, OBE, Assistant Test Pilot to "Mutt".**

small: Britain had more than 600 fighter planes to defend itself while the attackers had over 3,000 bombers and fighters. As July slipped into a glorious August, the skies over southern England became criss-crossed with vapour trails as the deadly aerial ballet exploded into life. The children of Southampton were, like youngsters along the entire coast, utterly enthralled. They watched in awe. They watched in excitement.

Young Ronald Lyons, the Southampton evacuee in Swanage, had an amazing experience. He recalls:

It was fantastic playing in the Purbeck Hills where we used to play Cowboys and Indians. One day we were high up at Peverill Point when we saw German bombers coming. They were incredibly low and we were actually looking down on top of them. I could see the pilots' faces and we all took aim with our bows and fired our arrows down at them. I swear this is true – one of my arrows actually hit the fuselage of one of them and bounced off! My brother Raymond also saw a Stuka dive-bomber crash land in Swanage. As it came down it was shooting at everything but when Raymond and the kids got to the plane, the pilot was casually sitting on the wing. He even offered his cigarettes around until he was escorted away.

The youngsters became obsessed with the warplanes and became more knowledgeable about their capabilities and technical specifications than their parents. They were also captivated by stories of valour and heroism in the skies. Then something happened over Southampton which brought the stories dramatically to life. An event which would be endlessly discussed in the playgrounds, in the streets and in the future. It was the day the children saw a real RAF hero descend towards them.

CHAPTER 2

The Swamp Boys, Al and John

Heroism above Southampton, August 1940

THE badly injured pilot floated to earth with uniform ablaze and blood pouring from the lace holes in his shoes. Although his eyelids were severed, he could see that his burnt and blackened left hand had been stripped of skin like blistered paintwork and the white bones of his knuckles were exposed. His right hand was also burnt and his foot smashed. An oxygen mask still covered the Hurricane pilot's face but his deformed hands could not remove it. He was contorted with pain. He wasn't quite sure what parts of

his body were working or indeed what parts were left.

Two young boys watched transfixed as the parachute gently lowered the shattered body of Flt Lt James Nicolson through a cloudless sky towards Millbrook. Moments earlier, nine-year-old Al Donovan and his friend John Hunt, 13, had been playing in "The Swamp" – the woods in Warren Avenue, Southampton, where local children built camps, swings and pretended to be Tarzan. Here the innocence of childhood was insulated

left: Flt Lt James Nicolson begins to bail out over Southampton as the Messerschmitt he hit plummets to earth. "Battle of Britain VC" was painted by Robert Taylor.

and protected from an adult world gone mad.

When sirens had signalled a battle was raging in the skies, the two boys had rushed to the top of Warren Avenue to get home. There, in the clear sky before them, Nicolson was lowered to earth. The pilot's ordeal was not over. A Messerschmitt tore past him and 23-year-old Nicolson shut his eyes and pretended to be already dead. He also anticipated the murderous sound of automatic gunfire to break the silence and end his life. Not a sound. He opened his eyes and the plane was gone.

The fields of Millbrook were now rushing nearer and nearer. Yet still his agony was not over. A man – whose identity still remains a mystery – spotted the descending parachute and thought a German was landing. He raised his 12-bore shotgun and emptied two barrels in Nicolson's general direction. The pilot was hit in the buttocks before the mistake was realised.

Nicolson at last landed in a field and the calm weather mercifully ensured he was not dragged along by his parachute. Now he lay there, his uniform smouldering, looking at the clear blue sky waiting for help to arrive. The events of the previous few minutes raced through his mind. He had been up there flying towards Southampton to intercept the enemy that afternoon of August 16, 1940. A large formation of Junkers and Messerschmitts had attacked the Gosport naval airfield and the Tangmere base where fourteen aircraft had been destroyed.

Nicolson, Commander of three Hurricanes in "Red One" group from Boscombe Down, had then seen three German bombers four miles away and been ordered to attack by his Squadron Leader. He had never fired his guns in anger before and had been disappointed when the bombers were instead intercepted by Spitfires and shot down. As he headed back up to 18,000 feet to rejoin his squadron, four massive bangs shook his Hurricane. Four Messerschmitt shells had hit his machine. The first had torn through the hood of his cockpit sending splinters into his left eye; the second smashed his spare petrol tank and set it ablaze; the third crashed into the cockpit and tore off his right trouser leg; and the fourth shell struck the back of his left shoe, shattering the heel and mangling his foot.

Nicolson had cursed himself for being

above: Al Donovan's back garden in Winchester Road, Shirley, with the woods of "The Swamp" in the distance. Pictured are Al Donovan (far right), next door neighbour, Brenda Lee and friend Bertie Downing. Behind Al Donovan is the family air raid shelter.

keeping the throttle open; it seemed to be in the fire itself and I could see the skin peeling off it, yet I had little pain. Unconsciously too I had drawn my feet up under my parachute on the seat, to escape the heat, I suppose." Nicolson had watched as the Messerschmitt fell out of the sky and gave it a parting burst before baling out over Southampton at 12-15,000 feet. Now, as he lay in the Millbrook field, he was unaware his friend Martyn King had also bailed out of his Hurricane during the battle.

The two watching boys, Al Donovan and John Hunt, had seen the second pilot, however. They noticed he was struggling. He was panicking. He was in desperate trouble. In fact his parachute had collapsed at 1,500 feet. King hurtled to his death, landing on the lawn of 30 Clifton Road, Shirley, where he died in the arms of a local resident. Mr Donovan recalls:

It was an incredible experience to see all this. We were in The Swamp, which was our home really. It had everything, a real fantasy world where we made rides and swings. We used to watch all the dogfights over Southampton from here and it was a thrilling experience for us kids. On this particular day in August I was with my pal John – I called him Jack. He was older than me, and my mentor, and he used to call me Nipper. When we heard all the gunfire in the sky Jack said we should go home and at the top of Warren Avenue we saw the whole thing. I can finally reveal exactly what happened to King. As we watched the men come down, a Messerschmitt came out of nowhere and shot one of the parachutes – the one I now know belonged to King. His parachute just collapsed. That's why he fell – I'm absolutely certain of that and always will be. I can still vividly recall looking across to Millbrook and seeing King struggling frantically as he came down. It was just terrible. He had been a sitting duck and the poor bloke was shown absolutely no mercy. He fell like a stone. Nicolson, meanwhile, was drifting towards Millbrook in the distance.

a fool but, as he prepared to eject, a Messerschmitt 110 appeared beneath him and loomed up in front of his gun sights. "Fortunately no damage had been done to my windscreen and the four sights," he later recalled. "I pressed the gun button, for the Messerschmitt was in nice range. He was going like mad, twisting and turning as he tried to get away from my fire, so I pushed the throttle right open. Both of us must have been doing about 400 as we went down together in a dive… I remember shouting at him when I first saw him: 'I'll teach you some manners, you Hun…' and I shouted other things as well. I knew I was getting him nearly all the time I was firing."

Fire had also spread in Nicolson's cockpit and molten metal dripped on his feet from the dashboard. "I remember looking at my left hand, which was

Nicolson had landed with extensive third-degree burns to his hands and body; he had wounds from shells and cuts from the shattered Perspex plane canopy; lumps of lead also lodged in his backside. Yet he was alive. Then, as he lay there, a commotion started around him.

Nicolson ended up taking the injured 'gunman' to hospital instead. An old Albion lorry then pulled up to carry the injured pilot.

Among that first group to reach Nicolson was a local doctor and his nurse, Sister Edna Brown, who were in a passing car and saw him descend. She later wrote to Nicolson's pregnant wife Muriel at the couple's home in Kirby Wharfe, North Yorkshire: "He was most anxious about his face … the doctor gave him a small dose of morphine to lessen the effect of shock. His calmness and bravery was simply wonderful and he seemed to me the very essence of the RAF – his first thoughts were for his wife and the coming baby and if his plane had come down clear of houses."

His Hurricane had in fact crashed near Rownhams while Martyn King's plane had fallen into a field at Lee near

A butcher's delivery boy, who had been cycling nearby, had started shouting at the man who had shot Nicolson. "Did you do this?" he demanded. When the man replied that he had, the lad started attacking him. The scene became farcical when an ambulance sent to help

right: Two photographs of Flt Lt James Brindley Nicolson. His colleague, Martyn King, was buried in Fawley Cemetery on August 21, 1940. After King landed in Clifton Road, Shirley, his ripped parachute hung on the chimney of Number 30. This grim memorial remained on the house for three months after the tragedy.

Romsey. The Messerschmitt shot down by Nicolson is thought to have dropped into the sea off Calshott.

A policeman based at Shirley, PC Eric Coleman, had also arrived at the scene to help the pilot. He later recalled how Nicolson's first concern was to dictate a telegram to send to his wife. It read: "Shot down, very slightly hurt. Full particulars later. All my love, Nick." The PC sent the telegram from Redbridge Post Office. In truth, Nicolson's condition was critical and he was given twenty-four hours to live when he arrived at the Royal South Hants Hospital.

That night in Millbrook, the two Regent's Park School pals, Al and John, discussed Nicolson's crashed Hurricane. Mr Donovan recalls:

I remember that Jack suddenly said: "I know where the plane is, Al!" Jack's uncle had told him it had come down near the Horns Inn pub in Romsey Road at Rownhams. Jack then went off on his uncle's bike to find it. About 10am the next morning, he returned and said he had found it and had a piece of it at his Gran's house. I went to see and there, behind her shelter, was a huge bit of the Hurricane's tail plane. Jack said he had simply gone in the field, taken it, and walked down the road with it on the bike. He even passed a group of soldiers on the way and they simply stared and said nothing. I gather the thing was eventually buried in the ground.

Other local boys were to claim they had taken other parts of the Hurricane. One boasted to have obtained the ultimate trophy – the fighter's gun-sight.

While the local children avidly discussed the downed aircraft, Nicolson was slowly recovering in hospital. His eyes were to remain bandaged for a fortnight yet he received a tremendous lift when his wife rang from Yorkshire to announce the arrival of their son, James. A nurse held the telephone for Nicolson as Muriel broke the news.

Nicolson's recovery continued at the Palace Hotel in Torquay, which was being used as a hospital. It was here that he

received the telegram that was to shape the rest of his life. The small scrap of paper informed James Brindley Nicolson that he was to receive the Victoria Cross. After reading the telegram, the stunned pilot turned to a pal and said: "Now I have to go and earn it." He later sent a telegram to his wife with the news. "Darling, just got VC. Don't know why. Letter follows."

Nicolson, who was himself fascinated by the Great War recipients of the VC, knew that only a handful of people had received the award since its introduction in 1856. He was filled with pride. Yet he was also concerned. Did he really deserve it? Was he really a worthy recipient? They were questions which weighed heavily upon him for the rest of his life.

In the short-term, he was a star. He was mobbed by the press, schoolchildren held celebration parties in his honour, and the Archbishop of York wrote how Yorkshire was proud of "its connection to you". On November 25, 1940, King George VI handed Nicolson his VC

enclosed in a leather case and asked him if his hands were recovering.

Little did Nicolson know that the King himself had decisively influenced the award. Indeed, His Majesty had privately expressed surprise that the exploits of RAF Fighter Command had not been reflected in any VC recommendations. Twelve had so far been awarded to other services during the war – but Fighter Command had received none. The King's concern was duly passed around the Commanders in Chief of the armed forces. Then came Nicolson's exploits over Southampton. It appears he had been in the right place at very much the right time.

Nicolson himself was tormented by the suspicion that somehow he had been politically selected to receive the VC. He always maintained that he had not earned it and others deserved it more. He felt a victim of circumstance, a fake hero, and a decorated fraud. Then there were the whispers within the RAF to contend with.

At first Nicolson refused to put the mauve ribbon on his uniform until he was reprimanded for being improperly dressed. Yet he somehow found the strength of character to move on. Despite his immobile, claw-like left hand, he was determined to fly again and justify the VC award – and that's exactly what he did. On August 4, 1943, he was sent to Bengal to command No. 27 Beaufighter Squadron. Nicolson insisted on taking the most hazardous sorties over the Burma jungles even though his left hand was permanently closed and his 1940 burns still caused him pain and sickness. He never complained of his injuries and proved an inspirational leader who was adored by his crew.

Nicolson later joined No. 355 (Liberator) Squadron and on May 2, 1945, left on a bombing mission to Rangoon, Burma, to soften up the enemy in preparation for Allied invasion. The sortie ended in tragedy. A fire started in the engines after 300 miles and despite jettisoning the bomb load, the aircraft plunged into the sea near the Mouth of the Ganges and sank within fifteen seconds. Only two survived. Nicolson

and eleven others were killed. His wife Muriel was informed on the last day of the war in Europe and, in October 1945, she again went to Buckingham Palace to pick up her husband's posthumous Distinguished Flying Cross. With her was their five-year-old son, James.

Today a stone monument stands outside Philips Semiconductors in Millbrook (the former Mullard electrical factory) on the spot where James Nicolson landed after his historic dogfight. The field that rushed towards him on that fateful day is now an industrial estate and Muriel unveiled the monument in 1970, the thirtieth anniversary of his baling out. Eric Coleman, the PC who had arrived on the scene and arranged the telegram, was also in attendance and he handed Muriel the original dictated note he had taken from her injured husband.

The Nicolson story did not end there, however. After his death, Muriel Nicolson was left with a Victoria Cross but no proper means of support as she struggled to bring up her son on her own. The young lad's clothes were provided by the RAF Benevolent Fund and his school fees were paid by a free bursary. Embittered by her circumstances, she began campaigning for a fairer deal for war widows.

In April 1983, in a bid to focus media attention on the cause, Muriel auctioned her husband's VC and other medals. The VC, a small bronze cross weighing a little over three ounces and simply cast, is intrinsically almost worthless. Its value, however, is in its rarity and Nicolson's was the only Battle of Britain VC. It was bought by Trustees of the RAF Museum, Hendon, for £110,000. The burnt uniform James Nicolson bailed out in was also donated to the Tangmere Military Aviation Museum where it is now encased in a humidity-controlled glass cabinet.

Al Donovan, meanwhile, one of the boys who watched Nicolson's descent over Millbrook, has never forgotten that day when the pilot landed. On August 16, 2000 – the sixtieth anniversary of the incident – he returned to the scene and placed a wreath at the stone monument outside Philips Semiconductors. Mr Donovan, who co-incidentally worked at the premises for 24 years, said:

I chose the same flowers for the wreath that would have been there when Nicolson landed in an open field. The day Nicolson landed will always be etched in my mind and I felt I had to do something to mark the occasion. I do not think history has been very kind to him either and that still saddens me. He was a brave man who unfortunately became caught up in the politics of the time. What a shame that his heroism has somehow become over-shadowed by something as petty as that. Nicolson was one of the men who served not only England but the world, for goodness sake.

History, indeed, continues to toy with Nicolson and the nagging doubt persists that he should ever have received the VC. Library shelves groan beneath the weight of tributes to Battle of Britain heroes yet Nicolson does not figure as prominently as one might expect. Instead pilots who shot down at least ten enemy aircraft bask in the glory, such as Douglas Bader, whose total score was twenty, and "record holder", Air Vice Marshall Johnnie Johnson, who had thirty-eight "hits". Meanwhile Nicolson, with his one famous hit, has been sidelined and left to wallow in the mire of political correctness from which his award apparently originated. This is grossly unfair. Nicolson may well have been a political pawn but it was not his choice. He was a popular, gregarious man and an excellent pilot who was himself tormented by the circumstances surrounding his VC. Further, it can be strongly argued that his deeds that afternoon above Southampton thoroughly deserved the VC irrespective of the whispers and memos circulating the corridors of Whitehall. The fact he managed to shoot the Messerschmitt at all while in such an appalling physical state displayed true valour worthy of the award.

Moreover, Nicolson combated his terrible injuries to prove himself deserving of the award in the years that followed. Even when the fated Liberator was about to crash in the Bay of Bengal, James Nicolson remained calm and reassured his men. He was last seen giving a thumbs-up sign moments before ditching. Then the shark-infested waters claimed the man whose cross had literally been too hard to bear.

Nicolson's landing in Southampton was endlessly discussed by Millbrook's youngsters during those balmy days of mid-August, 1940. Yet the month had begun with something rather different floating down from the skies. At first glance, it appeared as though it was snowing. On closer inspection, the sky was thick with paper which subsequently laid a carpet of confetti on the streets. They were pamphlets from Adolf Hitler, no less, containing a message for the people of Southampton.

Residents were supposed to hand the leaflets over to the authorities but they became souvenirs and quite collectable. Entitled Last Appeal To Reason, the leaflet contained Hitler's speech to the Reichstag on July 19, 1940. The Fuehrer blamed the "Jews and Freemasons, armaments manufacturers and war profiteers, international businessmen and Stock Exchange jobbers" for the war and then urged: "In this hour I feel it to be my duty before my own conscience to appeal once more to reason and commonsense, in Great Britain as much as elsewhere … possibly Mr Churchill will again brush aside this statement of mine by saying it is merely born of fear and doubt in our final victory. In that case I shall have relieved my conscience in regard to things to come."

Hitler was not, of course, interested in "relieving his conscience". It was actually time to start turning the screw. The main phase of the aerial Battle of Britain had begun on August 8 and three giant German air fleets – Luftflotte 2 in Holland, Luftflotte 3 in France and Luftflotte 5 in Scandinavia – began launching bombing raids involving up to nearly 1,500 aircraft a day. However they were soon to be badly mauled by the greatly outnumbered RAF fighters.

On August 13, Goering launched his Adler Tag or Eagle Day offensive against Britain. Destruction of airfields and the entire RAF itself were the main objectives. Goering had a tried and tested approach: bomb the RAF bases into ruins and wreck

as many planes as possible. It had worked in Poland, Belgium, Holland and France. "The defence of southern England will last four days and the RAF four weeks. We can guarantee invasion for the Fuehrer within a month," he told his men.

However the shrewd RAF chief, Hugh Dowding, kept large numbers of his precious fighters out of reach. He was an expert at feeding his limited resources into battle with care, economy and devastating counter-punch efficiency. Goering's Eagle Day was a disaster. Though he claimed five airfields were destroyed, the damage was negligible

and the Luftwaffe lost forty-five planes against thirteen for the RAF. Dowding called it "a miracle".

Some German bombers got through, however. That day, as Southampton families sat down to have tea, bombs hurtled upon the Old (Eastern) Docks and the Empress Dock. The International Cold Store Company was hit and destroyed after 2,345 tons of butter and hundreds of carcasses fed a fire that burned for two weeks. Many people still recall the reek of burning fat.

During the blaze, a dock labourer heroically volunteered to help rescue an

anti-aircraft gunner who had slumped unconscious at his post on the Store roof. William Fisher, 33, sat in a makeshift rope sling and was then hauled up by a crane to the roof. There, Fisher calmly secured the sling under the gunner's arms and watched as the injured man was lowered to safety. Flames now leapt around Fisher and shells were exploding everywhere. By the time the sling appeared again, he only had time to grab the crane hook before being whisked off himself. Fisher, an Air Raid Precautions warden, became the first Southampton man to be awarded the George Medal for his actions. Yet he was pretty modest about the whole affair. "Well, I'm naturally very proud that the King has thought my little job of work worth rewarding," he said, "but after all it was the least I could do."

The news was not so good a short distance up the road, however. In an area described as "a particularly poor part of the town" in the Air Raid Precautions (ARP) report, six people were killed as houses were bombed. Stores including Pickfords, Tillings, and Edwin Jones were also damaged as were eight pubs in the vicinity of Platform Road, the High Street and Canal Road which was still blocked for two-and-a-half weeks later.

Twenty-four hours later, on August 14, the St Denys railway line was hit and a passenger train derailed when a bomb crater opened up near the track. Two passengers were injured and another told the Southern Daily Echo: "The train stopped as though it had hit a brick wall...the driver and fireman had miraculous escapes." The train "proceeded to London via Romsey" according to the ARP report even though the southward line was blocked for nineteen hours.

The next day, August 15, the first

right: **Man and boy stand by the shelter which saved their lives in Endle Street, Southampton, August 23, 1940. A nearby shelter in the Chapel district received a direct hit, however, killing two adults inside.**

great battle of the skies unfolded when Goering threw the bulk of his planes from all three air fleets against the RAF. Eight hundred German planes approached the South Coast and launched four massive attacks. Aircraft factories around London were hit and five fighter airfields damaged. However, Luftflotte 5 met disaster. The Scandinavian-based German air group arrived off the north-east coast expecting it to be undefended. Seven squadrons of Hurricanes and Spitfires loomed over Tyneside with devastating effect and thirty German planes were shot down without loss to the defenders. It was the end for the Luftflotte 5 group and it would never return to the Battle. Five days later, when the outcome of the conflict was still in doubt, Churchill slowly rose in the Commons and gave history an immortal quote: "Never in the field of human conflict was so much owed by so many to so few."

Nevertheless, death was always waiting in the wings. On August 23, one Anderson shelter in the Chapel area of Southampton received a direct hit killing the two adults inside. Of the three others in the shelter, two children were miraculously unhurt. Then, two days later, during a night raid to the west of the River Itchen, a bomb ripped

apart another Anderson shelter killing a family of five. This was only a taste of what was to come as August departed and September arrived. Up to now, Southampton's raids had been casual, largely ineffective and carried out by small numbers of aircraft. Now, as September began, there was both increased regularity and intensity as towns and cities replaced RAF airfields as the main Luftwaffe targets.

It was a puzzling development since, by the end of August, RAF Fighter Command was near breaking point due to combat fatigue and loss of experienced pilots. The sheer numbers of Luftwaffe aircraft threatened to overwhelm the RAF and Britain at last seemed vulnerable and ripe for the taking. Hitler's dream of aerial supremacy – the prelude to land invasion - was within his grasp. So why, during those first days of September, did Hitler suddenly switch his attack emphasis away from the battered RAF airfields and step up bombardment of key cities and towns instead? It was quite simply a monumental mistake that ranked with Hitler's decision in May to temporarily halt his Panzer tank divisions as they advanced on the trapped forces at Dunkirk, so allowing the mass evacuation. It was also a mistake which would

right: On August 29, 1940, Southampton evacuee John Alexander had his own first-hand experience of the lethal skills of "the few". When Spitfire pilot Alan Wright of 92 Squadron shot down a Liverpool-bound Heinkel bomber, it struck the house where ten-year-old John was staying at Downton near Fordingbridge in Hampshire. The impact brought down the ceiling of his bedroom and broke his bed in two. Young John nonetheless survived and he returned to school as normal the next day. The German crew got away with slight injuries and the pilot complimented the Spitfire's good shooting before being led away to spend the war in captivity.

change the whole course of the war.

The chain of events which led to the switch began on August 15 when a German bomber dropped its payload on Croydon Airport in the suburbs of London. Hitler had specifically stated as early as August 1939: "The decision regarding attacks on London is reserved to me." Contrary to his wishes, the bombs were getting dangerously close to the capital itself.

There followed a second pilot error

and one which was to have historic significance. Bombing on the outskirts of London was one thing but hitting the city centre on August 25, 1940 – apparently unintentionally - was quite another. Hitler and Goering had good reason to be both furious and alarmed. They knew the British would retaliate against German cities. Goering, fuming at the ineptitude of those responsible, demanded to know which crews had blundered. He wrote: "Luftwaffe High Command will

itself undertake the punishment of each aircraft captain involved. They will be posted to infantry regiments." It was too late. Churchill had already made his views known on the possible bombing of London. If it happened, he had written, "it seems very important to be able to return the compliment the next day upon Berlin".

The next night, while Hitler stayed at his Austrian mountain retreat at Obersalzberg, the RAF hit Berlin. There were strong winds and thick cloud and most bombs fell in open countryside south of the city. However two people were slightly hurt in the northern district of Rosenthal. The one thing Goering had promised Berliners would never happen had now occurred.

More raids followed on Berlin. Hitler had to respond. To hysterical applause, Hitler told a women's meeting: "When they (the British) declare that they will increase their attacks on our cities, then we will raze their cities to the ground." He called his bombers off the RAF

right: German Stuka divebomber, renowned for its precision attacks on small targets, drops its payload over southern England.

airfields and told them to flatten cities and towns instead. The Hurricanes and Spitfires were reprieved and Hitler had effectively lost the Battle of Britain at this point – and also all hope of a successful invasion.

There was a sting in the tail, however: the Blitz terror was about to begin in Southampton and London. When September dawned, a large aerial map of southern Britain was unfolded before Hitler and his Luftwaffe advisors in Berlin. London would, on September 7 and 8, receive the most devastating aerial attack the world had so far witnessed, leaving more than 840 civilians dead. The city would now be attacked for fifty-six consecutive nights.

Red boxes were also drawn around other potential southern targets and labelled alphabetically from A to P. One of them was initialled 'I' and identified with

the underlined words "Flugzeugfabrik (aircraft factory) Southampton". In small print beneath the line it explained in English: "Supermarine Aviation Works." Hermann Goering's Luftwaffe was on its way to Woolston's Spitfire factory.

top: Devastation in Florence Road, Southampton after the night raid of August 25, 1940.

above: RAF pilots scramble.

48

CHAPTER 3

Douglas, Kenneth and the Parker Children

The Spitfire factory attacks and tragedy in Melbourne Street, September 1940

THE crumbling, yellowed pages contain two names which perfectly illustrate the cold, indiscriminate and merciless nature of war. One is Douglas Cruikshank. The other, discovered further within the musty volume, is Kenneth Henry Doswell. Both were aged 14 when the bombs which claimed their lives landed on the factory where they worked. They were just boys. Each child has his own thin sheet and the same typewritten heading appears on both: "Death Due To War Operations." The "War Burial File", hastily compiled at the time of the tragedies, lists young Douglas as a "shop boy" at the factory in question. Kenneth is also recorded as a "shop boy" who lost his life within the complex two days later. In both cases, the "Cause of Death" box is filled in with the words: BOMB BLAST. The stark documents also reveal that the bodies of both lads were identified by their fathers.

The name of the factory appears again and again inside the File as the location for the passing of young life: a

left: **Supermarine: Main Woolston Works, 1939.**

above: **Supermarine raid of September 15, 1940: The south side of the rail bridge in Bridge Road, Woolston, Southampton.**

16-year-old draughtsman, a 19-year-old typist, and a 17-year-old apprentice are recorded. Some had been killed within the firm's Main Works. Others had cowered in fear beneath a railway arch before it caved in on top of them. The entries continue with clerks, supervisors, toolmakers, electricians, labourers and riveters. They are of all ages, each recorded for posterity, each representing indescribable family agony.

The sombre tome was returned to the basement vault it had vacated inside the Archives Department, its distressing contents once again secured behind lock and key. Yet the memory of what happened to those it lists cannot be so easily shelved. Those recorded on the faded pages had been employed at the Vickers Supermarine plant in Southampton.

The linear factory complex, sandwiched between the Itchen River and Hazel Road, may well have looked like countless others to the untrained eye. Supermarine's Main Works at Woolston and the firm's Itchen Works a short distance up the bank of the river certainly looked ordinary. Just another two buildings lining the Woolston shore. However Hermann Goering knew otherwise. German intelligence had long established that within the walls of Supermarine, the Spitfire designed by Reginald Mitchell was being built. The elegant fighter was Britain's first all-metal, high-speed combat aircraft. It was unsurpassed as an interceptor by any fighter in any other air force. Therefore Supermarine, Britain's home of the Spitfire, had to be smashed. The factory was conveniently next door to the Thornycroft naval shipyard which

50

produced destroyers for the Royal Navy. Fuel depots, aircraft maintenance and construction facilities also surrounded the entire site. In short, the whole area was a prime Luftwaffe target.

September had already proved a tragic month for the citizens of Southampton even before the German bombers took off from their European bases en route for Supermarine. On September 11, eight planes had dropped sixteen bombs on the Cunliffe-Owen Aircraft factory at Eastleigh Airport. A new hangar was hit and workers were caught fleeing for their lives. Fifty-two people were killed and ninety-two injured. The casualties were rushed to hospital in whatever transport was available including lorries and bakers' vans.

Ten-year-old Brian Simpson discovered his school, Bitterne Park, was being used as a mortuary after the attack. He recalls:

All the local children went down there and peered through the gates to see what was going on. I remember seeing lots and lots of lorries going into the school and boxes and stretchers being taken out of them. The boys were saying: "Look — they're just in bits." No-one rushed up with flowers or anything like that as they might today. We were all pretty used to this sort of thing I suppose and the children just looked and then went home for tea. It was as casual as that. The school was closed for two weeks following that raid on Cunliffe-Owen.

Four days later, on Sunday September 15, it was Supermarine's turn. Shortly after 5.30 in the evening, thirty German aircraft led by Commanding Officer Martin Lutz dived from 7,000 feet towards Woolston. Twelve tons of bombs were dropped short of the Supermarine Works and Thornycroft killing six people in the nearby terraced streets. Thirty-four homes were destroyed and more than 1,000 others damaged to varying degrees. In fact the area was so badly hit that troops would later use the derelict streets to practise house-to-house fighting in preparation for the D-Day landings in Normandy. Yet only the windows of the Supermarine plant had been shattered. A high-flying Luftwaffe reconnaissance aircraft — a twin-engined Ju 86 — circled overhead and quickly confirmed the raid of September 15 had abysmally failed to destroy the Spitfire complex. The bombers would be back, with Martin

51

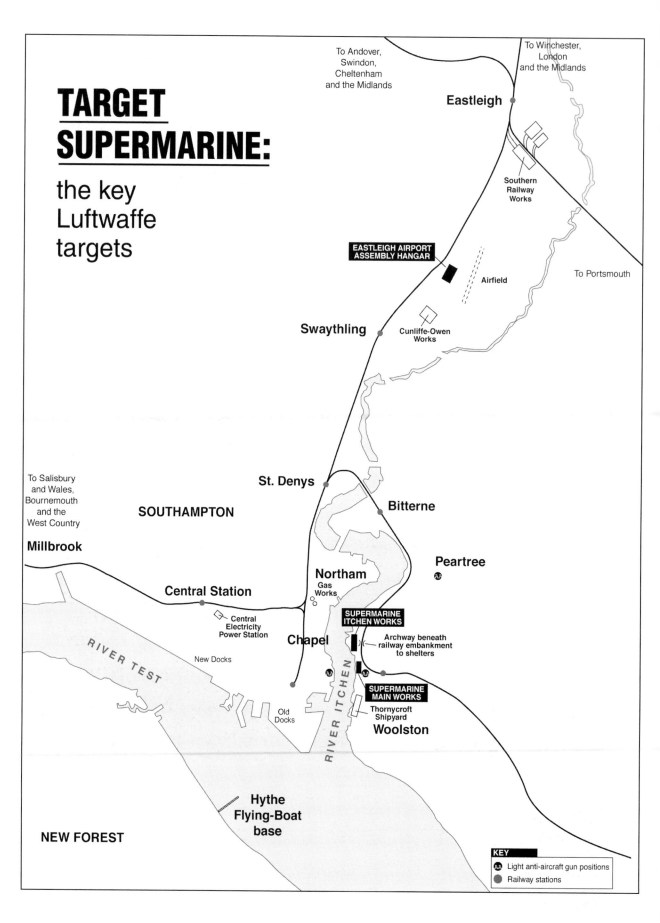

TARGET SUPERMARINE:

the key Luftwaffe targets

To Andover,
Swindon,
Cheltenham
and the Midlands

To Winchester,
London
and the Midlands

Eastleigh

Southern
Railway
Works

**EASTLEIGH AIRPORT
ASSEMBLY HANGAR**

Airfield

To Portsmouth

Swaythling

Cunliffe-Owen
Works

To Salisbury
and Wales,
Bournemouth
and the
West Country

St. Denys

Bitterne

SOUTHAMPTON

Peartree

Millbrook

Central Station

Northam
Gas
Works

**SUPERMARINE
ITCHEN WORKS**

Central
Electricity
Power Station

Archway beneath
railway embankment
to shelters

Chapel

RIVER TEST

New Docks

**SUPERMARINE
MAIN WORKS**

Thornycroft
Shipyard

RIVER ITCHEN

Woolston

Old
Docks

Hythe
Flying-Boat
base

NEW FOREST

KEY

AA Light anti-aircraft gun positions

● Railway stations

below: Martin Lutz who led the Luftwaffe Supermarine raids of September 15 and 24, 1940.

Lutz again at the helm.

During the afternoon of Tuesday September 24, thirty-seven bombers and escorting fighters approached Southampton and dived from 20,000 feet releasing thirty bombs on Supermarine, the Gas Works and the main electricity power station next to Southampton Central Railway Station. Lutz, who was

to die in action three days later and be awarded a posthumous Knights Cross, left a trail of unforgettable carnage in Southampton. Forty-two people lost their lives during the raid and more than 170 were injured.

After the bombing, one Woolston resident remarked: "There was a young lad who lived near me – he worked there

53

(Supermarine) – and had just started from school, really. And my small boy came in and he said: 'Oh Mum, Douglas is not home yet' – and this was well after tea. Anyhow, what happened was he was killed over there." That young lad was 14-year-old workshop assistant, or "shop boy", Douglas Cruikshank who lived in Osterley Road, a short walk from Supermarine. Young Cruikshank's friend, Mr Ray Penny, recalls:

We were both 14-year-old apprentices or "Handy-Lads", as they called us. We were both put with the aircraft fitters and were given odd jobs to do. At other times the men would play lots of practical jokes on us and send us on errands which didn't exist. I used to go to the shelter with Douglas when the sirens sounded but by September 24, I had been transferred to Seward's Garage in Winchester Road, Shirley, where Supermarine work was also being carried out. I was on the roof of Seward's and actually watched the raid. I was absolutely devastated to learn Douglas had died there. I remember his dark curly hair and glasses. I had the impression he was a very clever, studious type and he was certainly destined for great things in his career.

Mr Harry Griffiths, who joined Supermarine at the age of 14, was inside the Main Woolston Works that awful day. He recalls:

After my apprenticeship, I worked in the Laboratory at the Main Woolston Works. We were part of the

Design Department and work included the study of chemical processes, heat treatment, cooling, lubrication and advising on what materials to use. We realised we were a target when the war started but I suppose we had got quite blasé about the whole thing because nothing had happened – until September came around. Tuesday September 24, 1940, started as a normal working day, but just after lunchtime the anti-aircraft guns around us opened up before any warning had been received. Staff in the office block rushed down the stairs to the mechanical test room, which was partly below ground level, while production personnel left the Works and started to disperse in all directions. The Woolston employees scattered everywhere but the bombs were aimed at the Itchen Works up the road. At the Itchen Works, people started to go across Hazel Road and through a narrow brick arch under the

railway line to a row of company shelters on the other side at the lower edge of Peartree Green. The arch under the railway line received a direct hit and a group of employees was caught underneath. It all came down on top of them. Others had made it to one of the shelters built into the Works boundary fence and that was hit, too. The result was appalling. Many of them had been blown to pieces under the archway and others were very seriously injured. (Eyewitnesses recalled bodies had been thrown up on to the railway embankment where severed limbs poked out of the debris and mud; an ambulance man also recalled coming across the archway to discover the bodies had been transformed into a "human froth".)

The Main Works at Woolston was not hit in this raid and only one bomb hit Itchen works. It has been said that people would have been safer staying in the factory than attempting to reach the shelters by going through the railway arch. One thing is certain. The lateness of the warning saved many lives, as earlier evacuation would have enabled many more people to go straight into the path of the attack through the arch – or into the hit shelter on the other side. In fact, given earlier warning, I would have been in the shelter that was hit. Everyone who was still standing started to rescue those trapped and to help the injured. The Works-trained ARP organisation would have been totally overwhelmed without the assistance of the police, fire, rescue services and employees.

During the raid, the east corner of the Supermarine Main Works had received minor damage, a nearby railway bridge had been destroyed and unexploded bombs caused chaos which led to evacuation of the factory site. St Barnabas' Church in Lodge Road was also wrecked as were hundreds of homes. Belvidere Terrace in Northam was almost flattened and huge clouds of smoke rose above it.

Fleets of ambulances ferried the injured to the Royal South Hants Hospital in a never-ending relay. There was more to come. Shortly after 4.30pm, the bombers returned and twenty-five tons of bombs (forty-six high explosives) rained down on the Peartree Green and Radstock Road area. One more person was killed and five seriously injured. However, German reconnaissance was quick to reveal that Supermarine had again emerged virtually unscathed. Some workers who had escaped had actually returned to the factory the next day.

A third raid was inevitable and it came two days later on Thursday September 26, 1940. At 4.30pm, 120 aircraft attacked the factory complex in waves on a south-to-north axis. There was little warning. The raiders banked over Southampton Water and flew above the River Itchen before dropping up to 200 bombs – some seventy tons – on

both the Chapel and Woolston sides. Fifty-five people were killed. Seven bombs hit the Woolston Main Works and one struck the Itchen factory where it landed between two prototype bombers designed by Reginald Mitchell. They were wrecked and more than twenty Spitfire fuselages were also damaged. A propeller was hurled to the ceiling where it symbolically hung down like a large crucifix.

Outside, Supermarine staff ran for their lives as bombs dropped among them. Some workers pressed flat on the ground. The bombers were so low that eyewitnesses recall seeing the German crews looking into their bombsights. Maurice Young, celebrating his 11th birthday, was in his front garden in Merry Oak Road with his friends about one mile north-east of the Supermarine factory when the raid began. He recalls:

My mum had put a table out in the front garden for all the jelly and food and there were eight of us sat down eating. Suddenly there were lots of aircraft overhead. They were very, very low and I could see the crosses on the wings. I can't recall hearing a warning siren but I heard the Bofor guns that ringed the factory firing at the aircraft. There was a terrific roar and I saw the bombs tumbling tail-first out of the Heinkel bomb bays. The ground shook as they hit and there was a huge noise. Within a minute we

all heard the bells of ambulances and fire engines as they raced towards Woolston, and then the sound of our RAF fighters chasing the enemy. As children we didn't appreciate the horror of it all and one week later, after heavy rain in the low-lying area near the Itchen, we were swimming in the Carter's Field bomb craters.

Mr Harry Griffiths, who had experienced the raid two days earlier, once again confronted death inside the Main Woolston Works. He recalls:

This time there was more warning but most employees had lost faith in the shelters and made their way in all directions to get as far away as possible. The raid was heavier, with twice the number of aircraft and concentrated mainly on the Main Woolston Works. Another shelter was hit this time in the field beyond the railway. I was in the control room which was inside a building on the other side of Hazel Road to the Main Woolston Works but linked to it via a bridge. This building housed a treatment area on the ground floor and the Works canteen on the floor above. Everything started shaking when sticks of bombs began falling. We heard and felt the final group of bombs coming towards us and the last one fell on the woodmill building which was immediately alongside. It hit a girder at first floor level and exploded, taking away the whole of the canteen floor from over the top of us and demolishing one end of the bridge which linked us to the Main Works building across the road. The

above: **Aerial view of the smashed Supermarine Main Woolston Works after the third raid. The extent of the damage is apparent when this photograph is compared to the one on page 49, taken in 1939. Some bombs hit the river and skimmed the water in torpedo fashion before hitting the factory walls.**

56

right: Itchen Works as it was left after the third raid and above: inside Woolston Main Works after the third raid. The Woolston photograph was taken by employee Harry Griffiths who survived two raids on the Spitfire complex.

girder however prevented the rubble from the canteen falling down and hitting the group I was with. Steel doors were also blown open and debris came into the treatment area. The fuel oil tanks at the rear of the building were punctured so, with the risk of fire, it was decided to evacuate the girls who were with us. We formed them into small groups and led them to public shelters along the road. My group landed in the cellar of a local pub – we could all have done with a drink - but the all clear went so we sent the girls home and went back to the Works to see if anything needed doing. The Main Works at Woolston was badly damaged but it was the factory building and not the production equipment itself which was severely hit.

Up the road in Itchen Works, the factory was still full of fuselage shells which were later patched up. Some said we could have carried on at Woolston and Itchen even though the roofs had gone. It wasn't a mass of rubble by any means and the main walls were still there. (Many workers who returned the next day were amazed at how little damage had been caused in a daylight raid.) But it was obvious to me the whole manufacturing programme would now have to spread away from Southampton because the bombers would just come again.

Every year, when September comes around, I give thanks for the late warning that saved me during the second raid and a first floor girder that saved me in the third attack. Those raids have been in the back of my mind ever since. I don't brood over them but I can still see those people being brought into the first aid centres, all banged up and some with blankets pulled fully over them. The spirit of the people will always stick out. The next day I went back to work and, inside the fitting shop on the first floor, the men were throwing rubbish out and collecting their bits and pieces. They were singing their heads off. It wasn't bravado. It was spirit.

Woolston doctor, Mr Sakoschansky, had the task of inspecting bodies and confirming death during the appalling aftermath. He detected life in at least one man who had been put in an area designated for fatal casualties. That man made a full recovery. Meanwhile, as the terror reigned in Woolston, German bomb-aimer Robert Gotz surveyed the devastation from his Heinkel bomber 4,000 ft above. Gotz later wrote graphically of the experience:

The bombs drop out and disappear in a row into the slight mist. I photograph the target with my mother's old camera (see page 59)... those huge, systematically laid out industrial installations from which the smoke mushrooms up again over the whole area. What is really happening down there in this area looking like a drawing board? Clouds of smoke are throwing a veil over the picture, and above these clouds there are many barrage balloons sticking up undisturbed, like small Zeppelins. Suddenly there was another gigantic burst of flame, with a huge column of smoke following it — from an oil or gas storage

below: Maurice Young (left) pictured one month before his 11th birthday when he was to witness the third raid on Supermarine during his birthday party. He is pictured with his brother Harold.

above: **Young Ronald Lyons who cowered in the pillbox (see left) as a bomb destroyed the family home on September 26, 1940 .**

left: **The Lyons' pillbox in Chapel Road can be seen in the right hand corner with the baker's van on top of it. The remains of the Lyons' house can also be seen to the left of the pillbox.**

tank. Time to go and set our course for home.

RAF Fighter Command sent eight squadrons to attack the incoming bombers during the raid of September 26. Seven raiders were shot down but the aerial encounter only began after the majority of Luftwaffe bombers had left Woolston. During that third, devastating raid, the 14-year-old apprentice Kenneth Doswell, who lived in King George's Avenue, Millbrook, was among the fifty-five people who lost their lives. A further ninety-four were injured. As Supermarine's employees ran in terror, a terrible tragedy had also unfolded in residential areas on both sides of the Itchen River and down in the Old Docks air raid shelters further south. Mrs Pamela Moyse (nee Boulton) recalls:

I was eight years old and lived at the top of Woodley Road just behind where the Main Woolston Works was. During the raid, I was in the Anderson shelter at the end of the garden with my mum, Dora. My dad went outside afterwards and I vividly remember seeing him digging with his bare hands among the local shops to see if he could find anyone among the rubble. I also remember there were bodies and bits of

people all over the roof of our Anderson shelter. It was so, so frightening. It would be bad enough for anyone – let alone an eight-year-old girl. There was nowhere to run. We just stayed inside the shelter and prayed. It was such a ghastly sight outside and I shall never, ever forget it as long as I live. I still find it incredibly difficult to believe something as awful as that actually happened.

Across the River Itchen in the Chapel area, twelve tons of bombs had fallen within one-sixteenth of a square mile. It was one of the highest bomb concentrations the town would experience. Most of the twenty-one killed here were in four shelters that received direct hits. Two were Andersons and two were shelters at the Gas Works which itself was badly damaged. Some 800 homes were also hit and 100 required demolition.

Amid the carnage, as always, there were stories of lucky escapes as well as horrific deaths.

Young Ronald Lyons, who would soon be evacuated to Swanage, was living in Chapel Road during the third Supermarine raid. He recalls:

right: Also in Chapel Road, the wrecked Baltic Tavern. Ronald Lyons, peering out of the slit window in the pillbox, saw the bomb land on the pub and watched as its walls "bulged and caved in together".

It was a huge raid and there were eleven of us children living in our terraced house with our mum at the time. My dad was at work. We heard the rumbling first and my mum went to the front door with all the children to leave. Unknown to Mum, my brother Norman and I had hid under a table inside the house. My mum and the others had all gone to the pillbox shelter next to our house before she realised Norman and I were still inside. So my eldest brother Jim ran out and grabbed us under each arm and took us into the shelter. We had only been in there a couple of minutes when the baker's car

— I think it was an Austin — pulled up with loaves in the back. The driver, Mr Kate, came in our shelter too and then there was the loudest bang you've ever heard. A huge 500-pound bomb had landed on our house next door and the blast picked up Mr Kate's car and dumped it on the roof of the shelter. The shelter itself was shunted 10 inches (25cms) by the blast and the wheels of the car were still spinning on the roof when we came out. My dad was an ARP man at the time and he told us kids what he had seen. I remember he said he had found a pair of hands — just hands — on a gutter where someone had been trying to get away. There was nothing else left of the poor soul.

A cruel family tragedy had meanwhile occurred in a street close to the Lyons' family home. Something truly awful had happened in Melbourne Street and the commotion centred on an Anderson shelter at the home of the Parker family. Young Jack Parker, aged 13, was attending Deanery Senior School when he realised something was wrong.

A nurse had approached him and asked if he could see his brother Ben who was in the school first aid post. He discovered his ten-year-old brother on a stretcher caked in mud and dirt. Mr Jack

right: The photograph taken by German bomb-aimer Robert Gotz with his mother's camera. Plumes of smoke rise above Chapel during the third Supermarine raid. The Spitfire factory itself is out of picture to the left.

far left: Jack Parker's mother, Alice, who died in the blast. This picture was taken just before the bomb fell which killed her and five of her children.

above centre: Little Patricia Parker – a photograph taken a year before she died.

above right: Ben Parker who survived the blast with his sister Barbara who lost her life.

below left: The heart-breaking letter ten-year-old Ben Parker wrote to his father after the tragedy.

below: Young Jack Parker.

Parker recalls:

I cleaned him up because they were so busy after the raid and Ben asked: "Will you go and see if Mum is OK at home?" I walked home which took about five minutes and passed the car on top of the pillbox outside the Lyons' house. I noticed the Baltic Tavern was also destroyed. When I got into my road, I saw bodies being taken out of my house and neighbours stopped me going any further. My mum's dad took me to his house and told me what had happened. During the raid my mum, Alice, who was 30, had been in the shelter with my brothers Brian and Reginald and sisters Barbara, Joan and Patricia. The children were aged five, nine, eight, nine months and two-and-a-half respectively. My mum and all five children had been killed. So had a lady called Louisa Hooker who was 21 and used to help my mum with the children. I just couldn't believe it. I would have been in the shelter myself if I had attended school in the mornings like the others instead of the afternoons. The only members of the family left were me, my brother Ben who had survived the bomb, my sister Rita — who had been sent out on an errand moments before the blast — and my poor dad who had been at work and arrived to dig Ben out himself.

My dad went white overnight. He was absolutely devastated.

While Ben was recovering in hospital he wrote a letter to Dad — who was also called Ben — and it still moves me to read it. Ben wrote: "I heard that Mum is gone up to heaven and the children is gon (sic) to and I hope you dint cry. I dint cry, did you." It really hit me during the funeral in St Mary's Church. There were three coffins for the six of them.

My mum and the baby were in one, the youngest girl and the eldest boy were in the next and the youngest boy and the eldest girl were in the last one. You never come to terms with something like that and I can still remember the day of the tragedy. Afterwards, my dad went to live with his father and relatives looked after Rita and me. When Ben came out of hospital, the three of us remaining children were evacuated.

Tragedy also struck the Parsons family. Daughter Barbara Baker (nee Parsons) was 17 at the time and living in Pentire Avenue, Shirley. She recalls:

Down in the Old Docks, the corn granary was on fire after being hit by a bomb on September 26. There was a shelter beneath the corn granary and this was hit too. The firemen pumped water on the fire and that helped break the already weakened sea wall. The

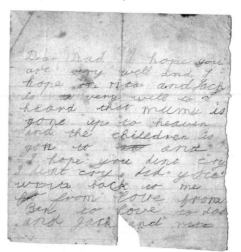

above: **Barbara Parsons** and below: **her father Jack who was killed in the Old Docks on September 26, 1940.**

shelter underneath was then flooded. My father, Jack, was Chief Pay Clerk in the Marine Department of the Southern Railway and on that afternoon he went to the shelter. Once all the water behind the sea wall came in, people tried to get out but my father went back in because he was a St John Ambulance man as well. He ended up drowning in there. Ten others also died. My father was in there for three days before they could get him out and they wouldn't let any of the family see his body. I had just had my 17th birthday and I had bought a black coat. My father had said: "Whatever do you want a black coat for?" A week later I was wearing it at his funeral. I was very sad. For weeks afterwards, every time the door opened I thought he would come back in again.

Back in the Chapel area, bus driver Len Whitwell found himself trapped alone inside his vehicle as the bombs rained down. He finally forced open the buckled bus door and ran to a surface shelter. After the raid, he returned to the wrecked bus to find the engine would still start. Len and his conductor then slowly drove their way along the cratered roadway before Len stopped to look at something in the rubble.

The late Mr Whitwell wrote about the experience:

What I saw made me retch. As I pulled the bricks away the space revealed the top half of a female human torso. The head and arms were there but nothing more except the remains of several items of ripped clothing. I left it there, spat out the remainder of the vomit which I had involuntarily brought up, then took my place at the wheel again. Not very far down the road I was forced to steer carefully to avoid a human leg; there was still a stocking and a brown high-heeled shoe on the foot.

Across the River, the carcass of Supermarine smouldered. Production was at a standstill and the plant was vulnerable to further attack. However there had been a contingency plan to ensure vital Spitfire manufacture could continue. In 1938, two years after Test Pilot "Mutt" Summers' first successful Spitfire flight above Southampton, work had begun on building a new "shadow" factory at Castle Bromwich near Birmingham. In the meantime, seventy-five per cent of Supermarine's work had been sub-contracted out to

about 250 firms nationwide leaving the Southampton plant to concentrate on riveting the new thin metal skins to fuselages.

Further safeguards were then put in place by planning dispersal of fuselage production. There followed requisitioning of Hendy's of Pound Tree Road and Seward's Garage and Lowther's Garage in Shirley. Hence, if the Main Woolston Works or Itchen Works were put of action, fuselage production could be resumed at these new premises at short notice while remaining parts were supplied by sub-contractors.

Prior to the raids, the newly built Spitfire fuselages were taken on lorries (known as "Queen Mary's") from the Main Woolston Works and the Itchen Works to a final assembly and flight-testing area at Eastleigh Airport. Here the Merlin engines and sub-contracted work was fitted and the aircraft finally assembled and tested. The finished aircraft were then collected by the RAF – frequently using women pilots – and flown to Reception Units to await delivery to air bases.

By August 1940, more than 800 Spitfires had been built since full-scale production had begun in 1938. Yet now, in the space of three horrific days in September, the production process had been halted even though vital machine tools and jigs (the steel structures used to exactly duplicate components) had escaped serious damage.

After the first raid on September 15, further premises were requisitioned. The process was simple, if unpopular. If businesses were required, the Local Government Requisition Officer would serve requisition papers on the owners – some of whom would be far from pleased. Two new businesses in Winchester Road – the Hants and Dorset Bus Maintenance Workshops (for wing building) and the Sunlight Laundry (to house Supermarine's fitting shop) – were now taken over. However, when Lord Beaverbrook, the Minister of Aircraft Production, visited Supermarine after the September 26 raid, he ordered a complete dispersal of the entire Supermarine complex. The fourth floor

left: Inside the Supermarine Main Woolston Works in 1939: wing assembly showing building jigs in the foreground.

of the Polygon Hotel was requisitioned for the Supermarine management team to begin organising the mammoth task.

Meanwhile, the design team moved to the University College of Southampton and the Commercial Office to a large house called Deepdene at Bitterne Park. A Master Plan, put in the hands of Works Manager Len Gooch, was drawn up to split the Supermarine work between four

left: Inside the Supermarine Itchen Works, 1939. It was here that the Spitfire fuselages were completed. The same assembly hall is shown on page 57 after the bombings.

towns, each using a nearby aerodrome. Southampton (using Eastleigh), Salisbury (High Post and Chattis Hill), Trowbridge (Keevil) and Reading (Henley and then Aldermaston) became the new manufacturing centres. Wing and fuselage assembly jigs were installed at each of the four centres so that these major parts could be married together at the nearby aerodromes. Detailed manufacturing stages were again subdivided and transferred to a large number of requisitioned local premises. Hence there were now four final assembly lines instead of the original one at Eastleigh Airport. The Southampton dispersal complex, managed by Arthur Nelson, was the largest of the four comprising of twenty-eight locations and employing 3,000 staff.

All did not run smoothly, however. Firstly, Supermarine's management disagreed with much of the dispersal plan and there followed problems in obtaining accommodation for skilled men in the new designated zones. Further, most of the parts used in the assembly lines came from sub-contractors and it became difficult to ensure correct allocation of components with some areas facing shortages while others had a surplus of the same item. Production gradually began to recover, however, and output at the "shadow" factory in Castle Bromwich helped to compensate for Supermarine's loss.

As a result of the bombing raids and dispersal, it is estimated that some ninety Spitfires – three weeks production from Supermarine – were lost from September to the end of the year. By September 1942, two years after the devastating raids, total output at the Birmingham plant had moved ahead of Supermarine. Hitler had therefore succeeded in driving Supermarine away from its original home during those harrowing days in September 1940. However he failed to stop the production of Mitchell's Spitfire or blunt its effectiveness in the air and by the end of September his final triumph over England had become increasingly elusive.

Ironically, September 1940 had promised so much for the Fuehrer. On the 7th, for reasons explained in the previous chapter, he had foolishly switched his bombing initiatives from RAF airfields to the destruction of key towns and cities. Nonetheless, late that afternoon, 625 bombers protected by 648 fighters launched the world's most devastating air raid to date on London. The capital was to be bombed in September by an average of 200 planes every night and almost 6,000 people died during these terrifying thirty days. There was genuine fear in Britain that invasion – the final implementation of Sea Lion – was now a real possibility.

However on Sunday the 15th – the day of the first Supermarine raid – Hitler's dream of invasion received the crucial setback. The day dawned cloudless and clear and Goering believed it was his chance to finally finish the job and pave the way for troop landings. He threw 1,000 aircraft against London but the bedlam in the skies that day marked the Battle of Britain's turning point.

It was the fiercest day of the Battle and one of the decisive clashes of the war. Goering had reassured the Luftwaffe that there were only fifty Spitfires left. In reality, German pilots confronted eighteen squadrons of Spitfires and Hurricanes – more than 200 fighters – during the first raid. Some 300 greeted

them on the second. One German Dornier pilot bailed out and landed in Kennington where Londoners ran out of their homes with kitchen knives and pokers and attacked him, inflicting fatal injuries. The RAF claimed 185 enemy aircraft were shot down. In fact the number was around sixty but it nonetheless represented the greatest German losses of the campaign. The RAF lost twenty-seven aircraft. It was "Stuffy" Dowding's finest hour – "the crux", as Churchill called it, and a defining moment which would subsequently become known as Battle of Britain Day.

Hitler now knew there would be no aerial supremacy and therefore no invasion of Britain. On September 17, the Fuehrer postponed Operation Sea Lion. He conceded: "The enemy recovers again and again…enemy fighters have not yet been completely eliminated…in spite of all our successes the prerequisite conditions for Operation Sea Lion have not yet been realised."

Valour and bravery in the skies had convinced a dithering Hitler that invasion was impossible. Yet the foundations for success in the sky were laid on the ground. That impressive bedrock was put firmly in place by men like Reginald Mitchell in Southampton. Mitchell,

above: Air Chief Marshall Hugh "Stuffy" Dowding. Douglas Bader, the RAF fighter ace, wrote of his former boss: "Lord Dowding is probably unknown to most of the younger generation. Yet it was because of him, as much as any man, that they have been brought up in the English way of life, speaking the English language. They might have been speaking German". Dowding died in 1970, aged 87.

left: Hermann Goering (centre with sword).

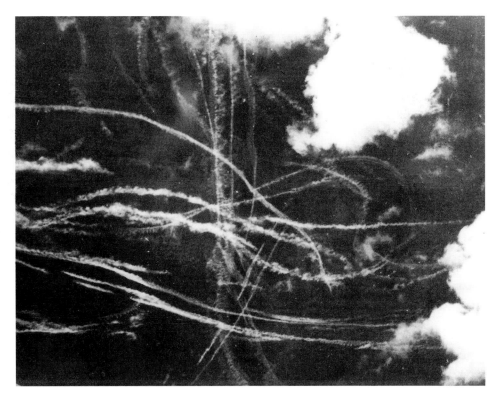

right: Aerial ballet: Vapour trails criss-cross the sky over southern England as the aerial clash rages. The children of Southampton viewed the aerial combat as a huge sporting event played out in the vast arena of the southern skies. They clapped and cheered every appearance of the "home side" – the Spitfire and the Hurricane. The mere presence of these aircraft weaving through the skies had a subtle yet powerful impact on the nation's morale. The sight of a Spitfire had "the power of a trumpet call", noted one contributor.

who was born before aircraft had been invented, designed the ultimate fighter capable of flying at over 300 mph. He died from cancer just fifteen months after watching his prototype Spitfire's maiden flight in 1936 and thus never knew his creation would be a main weapon in saving his country from invasion.

Mitchell – and Hurricane designer Sydney Camm – were not the only people who could offer the gift of brilliance at precisely the right time. Air Chief Marshall Hugh "Stuffy" Dowding, the Fighter Command chief, was an inspired strategist and pragmatist who helped guide Britain through its darkest hour and so helped prevent invasion; the personality, charisma and leadership of Churchill meanwhile unlocked and accessed the nation's psyche at a critical time with classic speeches urging resilience, passion and fortitude. In May 1940, he was widely disliked but by the end of the year he was a national hero. Then there was the inventiveness of others, like radar pioneer Robert Watson-Watt, which gave the RAF a telling advantage over a Luftwaffe which possessed no such comparable electronic aids.

These were some of the complex inter-related factors which underpinned Britain's finest hour and contributed to Hitler's fundamental anxiety and lack of conviction about the entire invasion project during those key days in September. Hitler's hesitancy in turn became reflected in an increasingly vague battle objective. Further, even before the Battle of Britain had begun, Hitler had one eye to the East. Thoughts of Russian invasion increasingly preoccupied him and, during the second week of October, he further called off Operation Sea Lion until spring – if then.

September, the month that saw Supermarine smashed, therefore marked a watershed in the wider conflict. The full, terrifying impact of the Blitz had yet to be unleashed upon the people of Britain. London would be bombed every day in October and a trial of blood and flames awaited the people of Southampton in November. Yet the aerial battle had effectively been won and invasion of Britain thwarted by the end of September, 1940. Southampton's Supermarine Spitfire plant – the physical manifestation of Reginald Mitchell's flair, tenacity and courage – had played a pivotal role in the victory. While the Luftwaffe wrecked the factory, Goering's airmen could not crush

the hope, imagination and resolute spirit embodied by the Spitfire it produced.

Today, only fading memories of those historic days in Woolston remain. The Main Woolston factory was never rebuilt and the site was cleared in stages during the 1970s before the Itchen Bridge soared overhead. An aggregate unloading wharf now occupies part of the former Main Works and a block of apartments has been built close to the old factory slipway.

The Itchen Works rose again – mainly on its old iron skeleton – and has been used by numerous companies ever since. Walking north up Hazel Road today – following the path the German bombers would have taken – it is difficult to see evidence of either the old Main Works at Woolston or the neighbouring Itchen plant as it once was. However there are tantalising reminders. For instance, an original two-metre wall still runs down to the shoreline where it now holds back a mountain of aggregate. A Job Centre further along was also the former Mould Loft where plane hulls were shaped. Then, bordering Hazel Road, is the overgrown railway embankment along which Portsmouth-bound trains run.

It was here, opposite the old Itchen Works entrance, where an archway through the bank once led to half-submerged, concrete shelters. Supermarine staff fled through this arch before the bomb that entombed them landed. The archway was filled in after the war when the ground beyond was brought up to the level of the embankment.

Back at the site of the old Main Works, a full-size Spitfire mosaic is the only tangible reminder of the past. Weeds have already emerged to threaten its appearance in Spitfire Walk. Opposite is a small, blue memorial plaque. The chipped surface mentions the raids and lists the aircraft made within the walls of Supermarine. It doesn't mention the September death toll – at least forty-two on the 24th and at least fifty-five on the 26th. It also fails to recall two 14-year-old boys called Douglas and Kenneth and five youngsters whose surname was Parker.

CHAPTER 4

Sing a Song, Brenda

The lull before the storm, October 1940

SMOKE rose from both banks of the river, eerily framing the slate grey waters of the Itchen. Youngsters had died. Families were fractured. Supermarine, the town's pride and joy, had been hit. Fear was closing in, its subtle forces teasing composure, draining confidence and unnerving minds. After the excitement and elation of the Spitfire Summer came the disillusionment that a long, hard winter of struggle lay ahead. A winter of cold carnage. A future of freezing, damp shelters and long treks to the countryside to escape the bombs. A future with less food, less essential services and less cheer.

However deep within Southampton's subterranean world, resilience, defiance and sheer courage somehow clawed its way to the surface. It did not require too much probing to find the evidence. Down in the gloomy shelters, musicians set up their instruments and performed to drown out the deafening roars of Blitzkrieg; cinema-goers clambered on to the stage and led impromptu mass singing when sirens halted the night's

left: **Ambrose and his Orchestra: one of the top 1940 bands.**

Fashion in October 1940: style ideas from Woman and Home magazine.

film; pub regulars, drinking watered-down beer out of jam jars due to shortages of glass, refused to stop their piano sessions for Hitler, Goering or anyone else for that matter; and nothing would stop teenagers from making the Saturday night dance despite many a ruined night spent sitting in shelters dressed to the nines.

So when the bombs fell, the music was simply played louder. It created

a barrier. It drew people together. It kept creeping fear at the front door. Entertainment was to play an essential role in the evolution of deep resolve, communal spirit and a determination to survive. People already had a common enemy, a shared ordeal and a united goal. Dance halls, cinemas, theatres and pubs now provided opportunities to further enhance and deepen that communal bonding. Unknown to those revellers,

such opportunities would soon radically diminish as the cataclysmic climax of the Southampton Blitz dawned ominously closer.

Yet now, once the September fires of Woolston had subsided, October had introduced itself as a month of relative calm in the town. While October for Londoners spelt increasingly severe night raids, the attacks on Southampton remained sporadic, even though an

Anderson shelter was hit near Eastleigh Airport on the 8th, killing three people. There was also considerable damage to property during the month.

However, on a wider scale, the month was dominated by massive RAF raids on Germany with Berlin, Hamburg and Cologne among the targets. October is therefore a convenient juncture to offer a further snapshot of life in Southampton, sandwiched as it is between the

Supermarine bombings of the previous month and the mind-numbing destruction of the November that lay ahead.

When war was declared, dance halls, theatres, cinemas and many public places were closed. The devastation that might be caused if a place of entertainment was bombed was too dreadful to contemplate and closure was deemed the best option. However, they had reopened by the beginning of 1940 and music and dancing became a way of life for thousands of Southampton's young.

Local church halls became dance halls where music was provided by small three-piece bands or simply by playing records. It cost about 1s (5p) to get in and local dance halls quickly established themselves as the most popular form of live entertainment. Venues like Banister Hall and The Pier flourished. The Southampton of 1940 also had large, established dance hall venues such as the Guildhall where the Bert Osborne Band and Jimmy James Blue Stars attracted big crowds. Some teenagers went dancing five times a week before rounding off with a big night on Saturday at the Guildhall where you could dance from 7-11pm for 2s (10p).

There may have been a war on, but the quest for the right image and the right clothes was relentlessly pursued. Men dressed up in their "fifty bob suits" and women wore anything from taffeta and satin dance dresses to smart and adaptable everyday attire that would be suitable for dancing. Shortages created fashion headaches and invariably led to improvisation. Coats were made from old army blankets, blouses from barrage balloon material and a whole range of more luxurious clothing from parachute silk.

For ladies with loose change to spare, there were also fashionable "siren suits". These were styled on the worker's boiler suit but were made of gas proof oil silk in a variety of pastel shades. Matching kid gloves, a silk scarf and a small "siren hand purse" completed the outfit. Siren suits enabled women, for the first time, to wear trousers in public without being laughed at.

Teenagers also bought "stocking kits"

to compensate for the real thing and sachets or bottles of "liquid silk stockings" promised to give bare legs the "elegance of sheer silk". A cream in a variety of four shades was applied to the legs and, once dry, a special pencil was used to draw a seam down the back. Many a row erupted in households the following morning upon discovery that the pencil marks had not been washed off and had ruined the sheets.

Various new hairstyles appeared. Pageboy and Old Edwardian – the latter being a mass of curls swept to the top of the head – were popular. Alternatively, a scarf could be wrapped around the head to contain the hair in a large roll. As many curls as possible was the basic rule and back-combing came into its own.

The dance floors themselves were the territory of expert dancers as well as young people looking for romantic encounters. The quickstep rapidly outpaced all others with the waltz and foxtrot following behind. New wartime dances such as the "Blackout Stroll" added to the mix. Venues like the Guildhall moved and swayed to songs which largely originated from the movies. The dance hall bands and orchestras in turn propelled the songs in the direction of radio.

There were many top bands jostling for supremacy in 1940. They included Ambrose and his Orchestra, Billy Cotton and his Band, The Billy Ternant Orchestra, Carroll Gibbons and his Orchestra, Jack Payne's Orchestra, Geraldo and his Orchestra, Harry Roy and his Band, The Joe Loss Orchestra and The Mantovani Orchestra. Many had their own signature tune (such as Joe Loss and "In The Mood" and Billy Cotton and "Somebody Stole My Girl"). The forces too made their contribution to the dance band scene with acts like the Skyrockets, the Blue Mariners, the Blue Rockets and, most famous of all, the RAF's "Squadronaires".

The big sounds of 1940 were sung, hummed and whistled in homes and factories across the town. The hits came thick and fast and included "A Nightingale Sang in Berkley Square", "Bless 'Em All", "Careless", "Fools Rush

above: **Corset advertisement: "Beautify your figure line."**

below: **The quintessential wartime singer, Vera Lynn.**

In", "The Lady Is A Tramp", "If I Should Fall In Love Again", "I've Got My Eyes On You", "Over The Rainbow", "When You Wish Upon A Star", the rousing anthem of 1940 "We'll Meet Again" and the definitive pub sing-a-long song, "There'll Always Be An England". A crop of singers destined to become household names were also being beckoned by fame. This illustrious band included Al Bowlly, Anne Shelton, Gracie Fields, Jack Cooper, Sam Costa, Dolly Elsie, Dan Donovan, Denny Dennis and, of course, Vera Lynn.

The provision of music in 1940 was not exclusively the preserve of big bands and big names. Far from it. Countless bands had been formed before the war and where individual members had been conscripted into the services, the "show had gone on" with new recruits. It was these bands that played in clubs, dance halls, factory canteens, garrisons and aircraft hangars across the country.

Music was perhaps the greatest wartime tonic for the beleaguered cities and towns of Britain and the children of the Blitz were providing some of it. Brenda Pritchett (nee Logie) was ten and living in Bassett, Southampton, when she decided to become a star. She wanted to be a singer and played truant from St Anne's Convent in order to attend an audition at The Palace Theatre in Above Bar. The auditions were held by Carol Levis who toured the country looking for young talent. Brenda recalls:

I went to the audition by myself and sang

"Glamorous Nights" by Ivor Novello, which was totally unsuitable for someone of my age. But I got through it and everyone made a fuss of me. By the time I was 11, I was doing Sunday afternoon singing spots during the prayer meeting intervals at churches. I was singing stuff like "Where My Caravan Has Rested" and "Who is Sylvia, What is She?" Once the war started, I was performing locally and singing at the big hutted camp along The Avenue, which was used for troops. It was all voluntary and I loved it. There wasn't much money about in those days and there was no television. So it was either go to the pub, go to the pictures or stay in and listen to the wireless. Hence any sort of free entertainment was lapped up and the Avenue camp shows were packed. I was in a concert party called Starlight Parade which consisted mainly of girls. We started off doing one show a week at the Avenue Hall and demand snowballed until we were doing shows every night.

I was still at school at this time but I had the stamina to sing at night too. But then St Anne's decided all the pupils should be evacuated to Bournemouth. My mum didn't want me to go and I went to Clough's College in Southampton instead to finish my education.

I then met up with two friends who were working at The British Power Boat Company in Hythe and I got in there as a typist. There was a concert party operating out of the factory called Laughter Express and they didn't have a female vocalist. I got the job at the age of 16 and my career grew further. We used to leave the factory as soon as we could and ended up doing three shows a week covering the majority of the South Coast. We performed in aircraft hangars, under canvas, in village halls and private houses, which had been taken over for the war. We were simply told where to perform by Southern Command.

I used to do the songs from the shows and the modern songs from that period. We had a routine and then members of the audience would say: "Can you do this for me, Brenda?" I sang songs like "Yours", "My Heart and I", "Stardust", "That Old Black Magic" and "Love Here is my Heart". Lots of them were Ivor Novello numbers, the most popular being "We'll Gather Lilacs". There were also the wartime favourites – "We'll Meet Again", "Wish Me Luck as You Wave Me Goodbye", " My Prayer" and "When the Lights Go On Again".

We always wore long evening dresses and tried to be as glamorous as possible even if our outfits were often cannibalised and made from bits and pieces. If you could get hold of a parachute you were in heaven – you could make lots of dresses out of them. With rationing you couldn't buy anything, of course. We

EMPIRE THEATRE
WEEK COMMENCING — SUNDAY, OCT. 6

HE ALONE.. *knew the Secret of Manderley*
SHE STRUGGLED *against the Secret of Manderley*

SELZNICK INTERNATIONAL *presents*

Rebecca

starring

LAURENCE OLIVIER · JOAN FONTAINE

with

GEORGE SANDERS · JUDITH ANDERSON

Directed by ALFRED HITCHCOCK

Produced by DAVID O. SELZNICK *who made*
"GONE WITH THE WIND"

RELEASED THRU UNITED ARTISTS

DAILY at 2.5 — 4.50 — 7.20

ABOVE BAR REGAL PHONE 6321

ALL THIS WEEK

Go Gay WITH Bing CROSBY AND Gloria JEAN *in the* LATEST COMEDY SING-SATION!

"IF I HAD MY WAY" (U)

Screened daily at 2.24, 5.23, 8.22

Also GEORGE MURPHY & JOAN BLONDELL *in*

CHOOSE YOUR PARTNER

Screened daily at 1.0, 3.54, 6.53 (U)

CLASSIC ABOVE BAR, SOUTHAMPTON. Phone 5200
Daily, 12.30 to 2.45 p.m. Last complete prog. 7.30 p.m. Suns., 5.30 p.m. to 8.30
TO-DAY AND WEDNESDAY
ERROL FLYNN, OLIVIA DE HAVILLAND *in* **DODGE CITY** (A)
In Technicolour. Daily at 1.5 : 3.30 : 5.45 : 8.2.
Also: The Riveter (Disney Cartoon). Latest News.

PALLADIUM Telephone 74712. Continuous from 2.15
PORTSWOOD Suns., 5 p.m. Open 5.30.
TO-DAY AND WEDNESDAY
CARROLL LOMBARD, BRIAN AHERNE, and ANN SHIRLEY *in*
VIGIL IN THE NIGHT (A). At 3.10, 5.48 and 8.26.
Also Allan Marshall and Barbara Reade *in* "MARRIED AND IN LOVE" (A). At 2.10, 4.48 and 7.26.

PLAZA NORTHAM AN ASSOCIATE ODEON THEATRE
TO-DAY and WEDNESDAY
CLIVE BROOK, JOHN CLEMENTS *in*
CONVOY (A).
SYDNEY HOWARD, JEAN GILLIE *in*
TILLY OF BLOOMSBURY (U)

DIAL 71555 Free Car Park ★ **REGENT** ★ SHIRLEY 5.30 to 10.15, Mats. Weds. & Sats., 2.15
TO-DAY AND WEDNESDAY
ARTHUR ASKEY *in* CHARLIE'S BIG-HEARTED AUNT
Also Charles Bickford *in* "ONE HOUR TO LIVE" (A). At 7.5.

AN ASSOCIATE ODEON THEATRE 'Phone 71273. **RIALTO** CON. FROM 5.30. WEDS. and SATS. 2.30.
TO-NIGHT AND WEDNESDAY
CLIVE BROOK *in* | SYDNEY HOWARD *in*
CONVOY | **TILLY OF BLOOMSBURY**
At 5.30 and 8.20 (A) | 7.0 (U)

THE RITZ BITTERNE. Tel. 3980. Continuous from 2.30. Sundays: Open 5.30. Commence 6.0.
TO-DAY AND WEDNESDAY
Basil Rathbone *in* **RIO** (A).
Also The DEAD END KIDS *in* "CALL A MESSENGER" (A)

SAVOY SWAYTHLING 74171 **SAVOY**
Daily 2 p.m. Sun. 6.
TO-DAY AND WEDNESDAY
Clive Brook and John Clements *in* **CONVOY**
(A). At 3.0, 5.30 and 8.5
CHARLES BICKFORD and DORIS NOLAN *in* "ONE HOUR TO LIVE" (A). At 2.0, 4.30 and 7.5.

WOOLSTON PICTURE THEATRE
Continuous from 2.30. Sundays: Open 5.30, commence 6.0. Tel. 68323.
TO-DAY AND WEDNESDAY
STANLEY LUPINO, PHYLLIS BROOKS *in* **LUCKY TO ME** (A)
Also EDDIE CANTOR *in* "ROMAN SCANDALS" (A).

SOUTHERN DAILY ECHO

SOUTHAMPTON EMPIRE
SIR CEDRIC HARDWICKE — FREDDIE BARTHOLOMEW
TOM BROWN'S SCHOOLDAYS
The COURAGEOUS DR. CHRISTIAN

GAIETY TWO PRICES ONLY 9's 1/2
JAMES CRAIG, LOLA LANE *in* **ZANZIBAR** GORDON HARKER, ALASTAIR SIM *in* **INSPECTOR HORNLEIGH**

FORUM
'BULLDOG' SEES IT THROUGH JACK BUCHANAN "BRITAIN CAN TAKE IT"
MY TWO HUSBANDS

PALLADIUM
EDDIE ALBERT, LORINA and ALLEN HALE *in* **ON YOUR TOES**

PICTURE HOUSE
IT ALL CAME TRUE
KNIGHTS OF THE RANGE

SAVOY SWAYTHLING FREE CAR PARK
FRANK MORGAN, BILLIE BURKE & ANN RUTHERFORD
GHOST COMES HOME
HONEYMOON MERRY-GO-ROUND

BROADWAY PORTSWOOD RD.
BULLDOG SEES IT THROUGH (A) | **MY TWO HUSBANDS**

REGAL CINEMA & CAFE ABOVE BAR Phone 6321
SPENCER TRACY and HEDY LAMARR *in* **I TAKE THIS WOMAN**
Also JOHNNY DOWNS *in* LADY BE GAY

SAVOY TOTTON
GEORGE FORMBY *in* **TROUBLE BREWING** CONGO MAISIE

CLASSIC ABOVE BAR, SOUTHAMPTON
TO-DAY REX HARRISON *in* **School for Husbands**

PLAZA NORTHAM AN ASSOCIATE ODEON THEATRE
TOD SLAUGHTER *in* CRIMES AT THE DARK HOUSE

★ **REGENT** ★ SHIRLEY
EVERYTHING HAPPENS AT NIGHT

ATHERLEY SHIRLEY
ANN SOTHERN, JOHN CARROLL *in* **CONGO MAISIE** NANCY KELLY *in* **JACK AHOY!**

GUILDHALL CIVIC CENTRE, SOUTHAMPTON
EACH SATURDAY 2/- **DANCING**

left: The cinema in Southampton during October 1940.

below: Stars of the silver screen, 1940: Clark Gable and Joan Crawford in "Strange Cargo".

above: Katherine Hepburn who starred with Cary Grant and James Stewart in the excellent comedy, "The Philadelphia Story". Hepburn should have won an Oscar for it but that year's honour went to Ginger Rogers instead.

only had forty-eight clothes coupons per year and a dress would cost five, stockings one and a coat around ten. It was impossible to buy — you had to improvise.

Then I had a very moving experience. I was going round the factory delivering a message and I saw a chap coming towards me. He was a burnt airman in his twenties who was visiting the place. I could see his face was terribly disfigured. His mouth was just a little thin line and he was smoking a cigarette through a hole in his cheek. I didn't want him to feel as if he looked out of the ordinary. I was determined not to make him feel different to anyone else because I once heard how one burnt pilot had killed himself after his wife ran shrieking into the street when she saw him.

In the afternoon I got a call to go to the personnel department and I was told it had been noticed I had smiled at the burnt airman. I was then asked if I would like to go and entertain the injured men at Marchwood where they stayed between skin graft operations and retrained for civilian jobs. These flyers had once had such marvellous looks — we used to call them the Brylcreem Boys — and were so young. But most of them at Marchwood had terrible hands and faces. When their planes were hit, the pilots or gunners in their Perspex bubbles would automatically put up their hands to protect their faces and the result was appalling. The evening shows for these men were the most important part of my wartime entertaining. I was only 16 years old at this time and I admit I used to have a few weeps when I was on my own. But when I was there I was OK.

The powers that be must have decided I was shock proof because they then asked me to go to D Block at Netley which had men with psychiatric problems. Some had survived a sinking or been in submarines and hadn't been able to cope with the depth-charging. They hadn't been able to walk away from it and forget it. They used to keep the lights on all the time there which was strange and someone would often clap in the middle of a number which was a bit disconcerting. But it was a real joy working in D Block. There was also a beautiful theatre there which made a real change to working in tents and the like. I think the shows helped for some of them because I met a sergeant later on who had recovered and remembered my performances. By now I was being recognized in places like Woolworth's, which was always embarrassing. I ended up doing 600 shows during the war in the end.

The cinemas — with the lure of stars like Clark Gable, Vivien Leigh, Ray Bolger, Nelson Eddy, Jeanette MacDonald, Judy Garland and James Stewart — also had

a magnetic pull on young people. With front stall tickets costing 1s (5p) and back stalls costing 1s 6d (7.5p), cinemas became the focus of the entire week for many. Al Donovan, the Millbrook "Swamp Boy" who saw Flt Lt James Nicolson bail out the previous August, recalls:

Sunday was the pinnacle of the week because everyone, and I mean everyone, went to the pictures. You had the Rialto, the Atherley, the Regent and all the town centre ones to choose from. At 6.30 or 7 pm, they would all amass in Shirley, all the blokes jazzed up with their ties and smart clothes and ladies on their arms. They would then get on the tramcar or walk. Everyone knew they were doing the same thing and all the talk was about this film or that, this cinema or that cinema. When you came back, the talk was once again dominated by what they had seen.

The cinema chains at this time were the Odeon theatres, the ABC theatres and the Gaumont British chain and all were cashing in on the explosion of interest generated by two particular American films in 1939. "The Wizard of Oz", starring Judy Garland, Frank Morgan and Ray Bolger, enthralled the nation and was destined to become a milestone in the history of cinema. The public watched amazed as Dorothy's house swirled in a cyclonic whirlwind in black and white before the Land of Oz miraculously appeared in glorious celluloid colour. "There's an audience for it wherever

above: **Dinneford's: a typical advertisement of the period.**

below: **The "Wizard of Oz" made Judy Garland a superstar in 1939. The film, starring Jack Haley as the Tin Man and Ray Bolger as the Scarecrow, has had the longest continuous exposure of any film.**

there's a projection machine and a screen," proclaimed Variety magazine. Indeed, it was the first time that most people had seen a motion picture in colour and cinemas across Southampton were packed.

"Gone With The Wind", starring Clark Gable, Vivien Leigh and Olivia de Havilland, was also released in 1939. The story of an egotistic southern girl surviving the American Civil War but losing the man she loved, was one of the most popular films of the entire war. Britain was not a maker of big movies in the pre-war period and so most home-produced material was shown to accompany the American "big one". Alfred Hitchcock's last English film, "The Lady Vanishes", with Dame May Whitty, Michael Redgrave and Margaret Lockwood, came out in 1938 and was arguably the last great English film before the war.

Most of the early wartime movies were therefore American imports. Then the writer and director team of Michael Powell and Emeric Pressburger began to make new, more realistic British films like "The Forty Ninth Parallel" and "One of Our Aircraft is Missing". David Lean's huge hit "In Which We Serve" was another archetypal British war film and effective propaganda flag-waver which introduced authenticity as a counter-balance to the heroic, America melodramas where one man was apparently capable of winning a war single-handed.

American film-makers hit back with a more realistic tranche of films of their own. One, perhaps more than any other, was of particular significance. The William Whyler film "Mrs Miniver" told the personal story of an individual family living in Blitzed Britain. Set in a rose-strewn English village, Hollywood presented an untypical family of absurd rural types in an untypical house of exceptional size. Yet the film, starring Greer Garson, Walter Pidgeon and Teresa Wright, was a morale booster and a huge box office hit. Mrs Miniver was even credited with strengthening American support for Britain when it was shown across the Atlantic. At the end of the

film, a vicar (Henry Wilcoxon) delivers a sermon in a bomb-damaged church. His now-famous words brought tears to the eyes across Southampton:

'The homes of many of us have been destroyed, and the lives of old and young have been taken. There's scarcely a household that hasn't been struck to the heart. Why, in all conscience, should these be the ones to suffer? Are these soldiers? Are these our fighters? Why should they be sacrificed? I shall tell you why. Because this is not only a war of soldiers in uniform. It is a war of the people – all people – and it must be fought not only on the battlefield but in the cities and in the villages, in the factories, and on the farms, in the home and in the heart of every man, woman and child who loves freedom. Well, we have buried our dead, but we shall not forget them. Instead they will inspire us with an unbreakable determination to free ourselves and those who come after us from the tyranny and terror that threaten to strike us down. This is the people's war. It is our war. We are the fighters. Fight it, then. Fight it with all that is in us. And may God defend the right.'

The cinema also offered pure escapism. In October 1940, "Rebecca" starring Laurence Olivier, Joan Fontaine and George Sanders was packing in the crowds nationwide and at Southampton's Empire Theatre. A vintage Fred Astaire and Ginger Rogers musical, "Top Hat", was showing at the Swaythling Savoy and Gary Cooper and Walter Brennan were in the moody melodrama "The Westerner" at Southampton's Forum and Broadway. The latter told the story of a "flaming feud of cowhand and plowhand" and was described as "the most magnificent outdoor spectacle ever filmed".

The Atherley in Shirley was meanwhile offering a standard war melodrama, "I Was A Spy", with Conrad Veidt and Madeleine Carroll. Charlie Chaplin also starred in one of his most enduring masterpieces, "The Great Dictator". Chaplin's satire on Hitler had a few funny

above: **Vivien Leigh in "Gone With The Wind". It set records for its length (3 hours, 42 minutes), Academy Awards (ten) and long runs (four years in London).**

below: **Fred Astaire and Eleanor Powell dancing to Cole Porter's "Begin the Beguine" in "Broadway Melody" of 1940.**

above: **Charlie Chaplin's "The Great Dictator" was first shown to the King and Queen, the Cabinet and representatives of the Dutch, Free French and Greek Allies.**

moments but the story of a Jewish barber being mistaken for a dictator was rather heavy going. It was nonetheless a big success.

Cinemas offered news as well as films. Newsreels gave the public an opportunity to get the latest information about the war and many were left with profoundly powerful impressions. In 1940, footage of European refugees and images of returning Dunkirk troops was particularly disturbing for many youngsters. Some even went home, secretly packed their belongings and waited for the call to leave the town believing they were about to be made homeless.

More suitable family-orientated entertainment was also on offer in Southampton. "Socials" were held at labour clubs and working men's clubs where games and craft activities were provided for the youngsters while the grown-ups could be left in peace to dance, talk and socialise. However, venturing out at all was not a particularly high priority for many families. Fear, the blackout, and limited finances ensured staying indoors was often the preferred option. Indeed, reading and listening to the radio were the most popular

pastimes. Television was also available to the British public as early as 1937 although only the wealthy were in a position to afford it. In early 1938, Pye was producing television sets priced at £40, which was astronomical considering the average worker's wage was around £4 per week. Around 25,000 viewers had sets in Britain but when the war started, television broadcasts abruptly stopped for almost seven years. The official reason given was to free much-needed technicians for BBC Radio but it was also suggested that short-wave television transmissions could help guide enemy bombers to their targets.

The Ministry of Information meanwhile imposed censorship on the media, barring mention of troop movements, ships, certain names and locations, new buildings or business statistics. For example, the Southern Daily Echo reports of the time – in line with their national counterparts – often declined to mention Southampton by name at all. The target of a particular bombing raid was frequently referred to as a "South Coast town" instead.

Prior to the war, the total combined amount of newsprint produced was in

right: **The popular – and saucy – "Jane" cartoon strip which appeared in the Daily Mirror.**

above and left: **The real "Jane" with dachshund Fritz.**

of reprieving the airfields and bombing towns and cities instead.

Selective reporting was also combined with cartoons lampooning Hitler and Goering but one item above all others caught the popular imagination – and particularly that of servicemen and adolescent males. It was the Daily Mirror's saucy cartoon pin-up "Jane", who was modelled on Eastleigh girl, Christabel Leighton-Porter. For a British culture renowned for its reserve concerning all matters sexual, the impact of this simple cartoon in 1940 cannot be underestimated. While Vera Lynn was singing lustily of a future rendezvous, raunchy Jane was baring all in the comic strip. Every day Jane and her dachshund Fritz were involved in a short adventure and, for reasons best known to cartoonist Norman Pett, she always managed to discard most of her clothing within a few frames. Bets were made in air raid shelters on what state of undress the heroine would be in the next day. The same meaningful conversation was echoed the length and breadth of the nation.

The Jane cartoon was first introduced in 1932 as light social comedy and Pett used his wife Mary as his model. Then, in 1940, Pett saw naked Christabel posing in front of a class of students at his old art school. "That's Jane!" he exclaimed and a revised, racier heroine was born with the blessing of Mrs Pett who preferred playing golf to modelling. Jane was unbelievably naughty for the times. Yet there was always a touch of innocence about it and her honour was never threatened, which crucially guaranteed both Jane's acceptability and universal adulation. Christabel, described by Churchill as 'Britain's secret weapon' and voted 'Britain's Perfect Girl' in front of a full house at the London Palladium in 1939, died in December 2000 after being diagnosed with cancer. Interviewed a month before her death, she recalled:

'Jane' became an important part of the lives of both servicemen and citizens. Even when injured soldiers and airmen arrived home, all they wanted was the Mirror. Submarine captains were even given copies of the strips weeks in advance so their crews didn't miss

excess of 24,000 tons yet this was now reduced to 4,000 tons due to shortages. The Southern Daily Echo during the autumn of 1940 averaged 8-12 pages, as did the Daily Express. A year later some papers had been cut to just four sheets. Yet the newspapers, guilty though they were of exaggeration, did much to boost morale. The headlines proclaiming the RAF's crucial aerial triumph over the Luftwaffe on September 15 are a case in point. Amid the flowing tributes to the pilots, the papers reported that 185 German aircraft had been shot down that day. "RAF Puts Goering in the Shade," screamed one; "Raiders Chased back to the Channel," stated another. In truth, the RAF shot down around sixty. Equally, the public never knew how vulnerable, how stretched and how precarious had been the plight of the RAF in August 1940 before Hitler made the strategic error

right and below:
Items from
Woman and Home
magazines, autumn
1940. This popular
magazine had a mix
of recipes, ladies and
children's fashions
– and romance. The
top story was entitled:
"If your husband may
not rumple your hair
then who can?"
The second item is
tantalisingly titled:
"Their kiss in front of
the fire."

out on developments. I posed for endless photographs and my picture was everywhere — in billets, barracks, mess decks, homes, even on the sides of planes and trucks. One week I even received sixty-two marriage proposals! I loved all the fuss and I began to star in West End shows as a result. At the time it was illegal for anyone to move around the stage naked — so I was pushed across, posing on a sledge for one sketch. It was quite a naughty show for those days and a chorus girl would stand in the wings with a fur coat for me. I lived in Wimbledon then and after my show I used to cycle the last few miles with the real life Fritz in a basket on the front.

While Jane won the newspaper circulation battle, magazines — costing between 2d and 1s (1p-5p) — were also jostling for market share. They included Women's Own, Good Housekeeping, Woman, Lilliput "the pocket magazine for everyone", Radio Times and Modern Woman which sometimes offered a special "Love and Marriage" advice section.

The uncertainty of the times and the resulting strain on relationships was reflected in these publications. While there had been an unprecedented

Their kiss in front of the fire was long and sweet. "You knew that had to be, didn't you?" he said.

increase in weddings in 1940, young single women asked magazine agony aunts whether they should sleep with their boyfriends. "Why shouldn't we have this happiness before he goes away?" was a common question. The response was stern, moral and to the point. The virtues of patience and responsibility were consistently preached with one magazine suggesting: "The emotions of which you speak may well be the result of excitement and unnatural tension."

There were no such moral dilemmas in another sector of the market. While comics for younger children — such as Tiny Tots, The Wizard, The Beano and The Rainbow — steered clear of war stories, the heroes of the Battle of Britain featured in those aimed at their elders. The Hotspur, The Champion, Boy's Own Paper, Meccano Magazine, Air Stories and The Rover were packed with blazing Luftwaffe aircraft and British gallantry. Boy's Own Paper also contained advice on how youngsters could help the war effort. An article on assisting the ARP (Air Raid Precautions) to ensure an effective blackout suggested: "Occasionally do a round of the houses after dark, looking for light spots that require fresh attention." The comic Girls' Crystal meanwhile offered a war theme for girls with stories featuring female endeavour, outstanding bravery against the enemy, and coy, admiring glances at dashing RAF pilots.

"HAVE THESE CHILDREN BEEN EVACUATED?"
"NOT YET SIR—I'M JUST MIXING THEM UP A DOSE!"

left: Comic postcards featuring children. They were a good way to communicate and also caused a chuckle.

far left: The popular Boy's Own Paper.

Back in the real world, the radio or "wireless" was the essential link between the British people and the world at war. Most radios were battery operated, the power coming from a wet cell battery known as an "accumulator" that often had to be taken to a radio shop or a technician to be re-charged or replaced. The bulletins began at 7am and continued mostly on the hour with those at 6pm and 7pm being religiously listened to by the whole family.

From Churchill's speeches to the latest information on rules and regulations, the radio became an absolute necessity in every household.

In 1939, the BBC merged all their programmes and broadcast on one wavelength, the BBC Home Service. Later in the year, pressure was mounting to provide alternative programmes and in February 1940 the Forces Programme began broadcasting every day between 11am and 11pm. The Forces Programme became a huge hit with its offering of dance music, show clips and personality interviews. The Home Service responded by attempting to be more accessible and less stuffy. News readers now introduced themselves by name and began to realise their own personalities could alone pull in listeners. Some radio voices became instantly recognizable: news readers like Bruce Belfrage, John Snagge and Freddie Grisewood almost became part of the

KEEP IT DARK—
I'LL BE SEEING YOU SOON!

family.

Thousands also tuned in to certain broadcasts. Liverpool-born comic Tommy Handley was one of the biggest stars with the biggest BBC salary – about £320 a week. His ITMA programme ("It's That Man Again") was a successful mix of absurdity, nonsense and satire, which spawned several catchphrases that were repeated in schools and homes across Britain. The most famous were "Can I do yer now, sir?" (which meant "It's your turn, now") and "I don't mind if I do". The show also introduced a host of popular characters – many of whom are still remembered today – such as cockney charwoman Mrs Mopp, blustering Colonel Chinstrap and Fusspot the civil servant.

Other radio stars included Arthur Askey

TRIUMPH 2⁰
very Tuesday

ALL TOGETHER
BOYS!

WE WANT THE TRIUMPH! CAN YOU HEAR
US, NEWSAGENTS!

THE TRIUMPH AND GEM

above and right: **Boys' favourite comics featuring British heroics over the hapless Germans.**

by dance bands, orchestras and military bands for the entertainment of millions of workers around Britain, twice a day. Some 8,000 larger factories even piped the music through to their workers and it's estimated that four-and-a-half million staff tuned in every day together with another ten million at home.

For youngsters, "Children's Hour" was a must with the reassuring voice of "Uncle Mac" (Derek McCulloch) behind the microphone. Millions will never forget the same soothing, closing words with which he concluded each broadcast: "Goodnight children, everywhere."

Southampton, meanwhile, offered other attractions for young people. The famous Lido pool, with its stone terraces, had been packed with sunbathers that summer; the Pier had provided the ideal place for people watching; the Sportsdrome ice rink in Banister Road had also hosted shows including one by the great Champion of the World, Sonja Henie; the nearby speedway track at Banister Court was popular; and the Saints could be watched at the Dell where admission cost 1s (5p) to watch a "Section South" football league match.

Young people were also doing their bit for the war effort. In common with other towns and cities, Southampton had launched a Spitfire Fighter Fund, a public appeal for cash to help finance the

– with his horned rimmed spectacles and "Hello Playmates!" greeting – and the rather bizarre "Radio Doctor", Charles Hill. In a very deep tone, he would offer such gems as: "Good day to you. This is your radio doctor. Are you feeling a little off colour? You can still feel the dinner that you ate two hours ago, you're tired, listless, you can hear constant banging? No, it's not another air raid, it's your head throbbing…" It wasn't meant to be comedy but the doctor's strange, monotonous diatribe was loved by the British public. Ratings went through the roof.

Another popular programme was "The Brains Trust", first broadcast in 1941. The show employed a question and answer format where the "brains" – eminent philosopher Professor Cyril Joad, scientist Julian Huxley and Commander A.B. Campbell – answered questions sent in by listeners.

By Autumn 1940, the BBC's "Music While You Work" programme was well established. It played instrumental music

ROCKFIST ROGAN. R.A.F.

THE CHAMPION AND TRIUMPH

3⁰

LEADER OF THE LOST COMMANDOS.

79

aircraft's manufacture. The Southern Daily Echo columns cunningly emphasised the contribution of schoolchildren who raised cash by selling treasured toys or by becoming ingenious entrepreneurs. Parental contributions often guiltily followed. One eight-year-old raised 11s (55p) by selling two bath towels to neighbours; two 11-year-olds sold their chocolate bars; a brother and sister sold pears from their garden; and, "using oddments of wool", two girls made moth ball bags and sold them at 2d (1p) each.

Whole schools became involved in the fund-raising effort and adults, continually reminded of their children's sacrifice, soon made up the deficit. By the end of October 1940, more than £15,000 had been collected in the town. The Echo Editor concluded: "And so now Southampton, birthplace and home of the Spitfire, can claim to have raised the price of three Spitfires and to have created a fitting memorial to a former townsman, the late Mr R J Mitchell, who designed one of the most successful types of fighter aircraft the world has seen."

Yet now grey November beckoned. The storm clouds were gathering. The bombers were on their way again. Those laughing and singing in the theatres, cinemas, dance halls and pubs of Southampton would now experience the full, destructive power of Blitzkrieg. On October 12, Hitler had put Operation Sea Lion on the back-burner until at least the spring – if then. Further, on the last day of October, the Luftwaffe's period of intensive night bombing also effectively ended. It was a moment which historians would later define as the technical end of the Battle of Britain.

However, it was far from over for Southampton. The Luftwaffe's orders were clear enough: leave Britain's premier southern port in ashes. The time had finally come. No-one could be spared. Not even children.

left: **Children praised in the Southern Daily Echo for their contribution to the town's Spitfire Fund.**

CHAPTER 5

"They are coming, Pat ..."

The Art School bombing and horror at the Garibaldi pub, November 6 and 23, 1940

INSIDE the white chamber it's almost possible to hear their little voices. Desperate, inhuman sounds. Unbearable, sickening images. Tiny bodies broken, burnt and distorted beyond recognition. The lives of young girls draining away. Then the words etched on the chamber's white walls attack the senses, painting new, disturbing pictures and inviting further, harrowing contemplation.

It's possible to feel like an unwelcome intruder. It is equally possible to feel strangely drawn, held and then transfixed. High above, light streams through

a square window, toying with the calligraphy sculptured in relief. Six tiny pink bulbs also cast upward light upon the script. High on the wall immediately ahead are the large words written in capital letters: "THE SIRENS SOUNDED".

Turning to the wall on the right, there is more, again carved in relief upon the white surface: "LOOKED EXACTLY LIKE A LADDER FALLING FROM THE PLANE. WE FELT A TREMENDOUS SHUDDERING OF THE BUILDING."

Turning again to face the entrance, more words appear over the top of

left: Devastation outside the entrance to the Art Gallery, November 6, 1940. The bombed Art School, where young children died, was situated out of view further right on the corner of the frontage.

the stone archway: "THAT QUICK MEMORY HAS STAYED WITH ME IN ALL ITS VIVIDNESS. I LOST SOME OF MY CLASSMATES. IT WAS A TERRIBLE DAY FOR US ALL." The final wall states: "THESE ARE THE ONES I CRY FOR EVERY REMEMBRANCE DAY."

Beneath are two columns, each containing nine names.

The memorial chamber, just inside the entrance to Southampton City Art Gallery, remembers the victims of a bombing raid which numbed Southampton. A short distance away, deep down within a basement labyrinth of dark rooms

EILEEN BARTLETT	DAISY MERCER
THELMA FRY	BETTY DAVIES
PAMELA BLACKFORD	SHEILA ROUTLEDGE
BRENDA HAMBRIDGE	HILDA DICK
EMMA BOYD	FREDA SHEATH
HORACE HARVEY	NORA EDSON
GEORGE BROWN	SHEILA STOCKWELL
GRACE LANHAM	THELMA EDWARDS
ESME CALWOOD	VIOLET WEBB

and corridors, was where the nightmare occurred. With this knowledge, it's difficult not to look down. The wooden floor can become a looking glass and the resulting imaginary flashbacks are too unsettling, too unpleasant to receive for long.

It's equally difficult to comprehend the mind of the man who derived particular satisfaction from what happened here. Luftwaffe chief Hermann Goering had observed how the town's Civic Centre complex – which housed a new Art Gallery opened just eighteen months earlier by the Duke and Duchess of Gloucester – looked like a cake from the air. He now vowed "to cut himself a slice". When his bombers droned overhead on November 6, 1940, children were working inside the School of Art situated on the corner of the new Art Gallery block. Fifteen children, including some from the local orphanage in King's Park Road, were pupils of the Central District Girls' School and aged between 11 and 13. The Central youngsters had been attending for only a couple of weeks and an afternoon needle and thread session was in progress when the bomb doors opened above.

right: The wrecked
Art School beneath
which 14 children
were killed inside
an underground
basement shelter.

At 2.45pm precisely, twelve bombs fell
from the sky for their appointment with
the innocents of war. One of the 500-
pound explosives dropped directly on
the School of Art. The bomb penetrated
the roof and smashed through two
floors, obliterating the School of Art
classrooms and exploding in a basement
shelter where the Central youngsters
and teachers were hiding. It was the first
time the children had been to the shelter
which was, more correctly, simply a
basement area lined with central heating
pipes. It had not been properly prepared
as a shelter. Fourteen children from
Central District Girls' School were killed
when the bomb detonated inside their
enclosed tomb. A further twenty-one
people – including a bedridden boy and
other Art School pupils – died in and
around the Civic Centre complex. Many
of the Central youngsters were badly
disfigured by burns from the basement
blast or crushed by falling debris. Others
were burned after the central heating
pipes lining the basement walls exploded,
shooting scalding water over the trapped
occupants. Just one child from Central
District Girls' School, 13-year-old Audrey
Hunt, survived the shelter horror.

A black folder, resting on a wooden
podium inside the entrance to the
white memorial chamber, contains the
disturbing details of that fateful day. It
reveals that two of the names listed high
on the wall – Horace Harvey and Daisy
Mercer – were staff. Horace Harvey was
an archaeology teacher and Deputy
Headmaster of the School of Art. Daisy
Mercer taught dress design. Two other
names belong to Civic Centre staff:
George Brown, the "Town Sergeant",
and Grace Lanham, listed as "wife of
the Superintendent". The remaining
fourteen names on the wall belong to
those children from Central District Girls'
School who died.

The black folder contains several
letters from survivors and witnesses
of the raid sent to the City Council.
They were requested to help plan the
memorial (which was opened in 1994)
and the poignant sentences on the walls
have been selected from these written
submissions. When read collectively, these
accounts make a moving and profoundly
sad impression. The selected extracts
which follow are printed as they are
written in the folder. Leonard Daniels
wrote:

*You probably know that I was in the then arts school
when the bombs fell. There had been many false
alarms, and it had been agreed that younger students
should go at once to the shelters when there was an
air raid warning, but adult students might continue*

above: One of the Luftwaffe's most famous fighter aces, Helmut Wick, was in action over Southampton that tragic day, November 6, 1940. He claimed several Spitfire and Hurricane "hits" on his return journey. Wick was lost in action later in the month – after claiming his 56th victory.

to work if they wished. So it was that a group of my students continued in their painting room and, by extraordinary good luck, escaped serious hurt. We were all rather shaken up. It was <u>very</u> sad that so many in the proper shelter were killed or very badly injured.

A sister of victim Sheila Stockwell, J Anderson, wrote:

I was working at the time in the office of Walpole Dispensary which was just across the parks on the corner of East Park Terrace, so heard the bomb drop but didn't know what had happened until I arrived home. I also helped identify her at the South Hants Hospital, which was very difficult, as they were burnt to a cinder.

Another letter is from B Beedon (nee Atherton), who was at Central District Girls' School in Argyle Road, Southampton, that day. She states:

I remember the Art Gallery being bombed that afternoon as I and my class were in the air raid shelter of the Central District Girls' School. I lost some of my classmates that afternoon, the girl I sat next to, also the one in front of me, and other girls in the class. I was in B6; girls in 7A were lost too.

Meanwhile, Honor Furslinheim (nee Blackley) recalls the heartbreaking sounds of human suffering inside the bombed School of Art:

I had woken that morning thinking that it would be a happy day – November 6, 1940 was my 19th birthday – but the afternoon was filled with horror. A few of us were painting in one of the main studios in the brand new School of Art of which everyone was so proud. The air raid warning went but we had had several false alarms earlier and decided to go on with our work. Two minutes later we were lying under the tables while plaster and pieces of glass rained down upon us. We decided, belatedly, to go down to the shelter – but then we realised that it was the shelter itself which had been hit. A huge wall of debris prevented our getting near it. From beyond this wall, we could hear the screams of those who were inside. Rescue teams arrived and we were told to leave as there was nothing we could do. Outside in the forecourt we learned that many students had been killed...

John Guilmant describes the raid in his letter:

I was on the steps of the Guildhall that fateful Wednesday afternoon and had seen the bomber which looked like an English Wellington. Suddenly I saw two silvery fish coming from the sky. I was standing between the second and third pillars when suddenly there was a terrible explosion nearby. I had fallen but picked myself up to rush towards the arts centre. The corner and walls had crumbled and water was gushing out of the pipes. Clambering over the masonry, I was called back by the heavy rescue team which had arrived very quickly and we were told to leave the area. That quick memory has stayed with me in all its vividness.

Audrey Lanham, daughter of Percy and Grace Lanham, wrote about the death of her mother in the complex:

My mother was killed in this raid. My father was Superintendent of the Civic Centre and he, my mother and I lived in a flat which was adjacent to the basement air raid shelter. On this day my father had just left the flat when the German plane, which was in difficulties, began to jettison its bombs. My mother and I were just about to make our way to the shelter, where we had taken refuge on a number of previous occasions, when the bombs exploded. I was buried in rubble up to my waist and could not move. There was total darkness for some time owing to the density of the dust. After what seemed to me an eternity, but in fact was only a few minutes, my father arrived and then other people who eventually managed to free me and I was taken to the Royal South Hants Hospital with a suspected broken leg, but which turned out to be only dislocated. During the time I was trapped in the rubble there was no sign of my mother and, in spite of my repeated calls to her, there was no response. It was some time later that her body was found.

Mrs Grace Lloyd, who was 21 at the time, wrote:

I witnessed the bombs fall on that afternoon from a vantage point in the Residential Hostel at the bottom of Hill Lane. The bombs in question looked exactly like a LADDER falling from the plane, not single bombs…

Finally Patricia Milford Evans, who was aged ten and in a wheelchair, offers one of the most moving accounts of all:

…My grandmother had taken me on the bus in my wheelchair. I was unable to walk. We crossed at the park to go to the Civic Centre. A civil defence man with a walkie-talkie spoke to my grandmother. He told her not to go into the building because of an expected air raid. He said: "They left Portsmouth twenty minutes ago. The Air Raid Siren should sound at any minute. They are dropping incendiary bombs today. I advise you not to go into that building with a wheelchair. It will be safer to stay out of it." My grandmother insisted…

below: **The injured are carried away after the Art Gallery raid, November 6, 1940.**

above: **New Road, Southampton, November 6, 1940.**

She left me just inside an exit at the end of a long, wide corridor. She had no sooner gone than the bombs started dropping on the building. First one came, and I heard that one. The impact after was of more than one, and I was temporarily unable to hear clearly. The walls opposite shook, then bulged. The lights went out at the first impact. It was dark but one could see sufficiently well. Next, I was amazed

to see all the paint from the beautiful pictures lift, blister and run down the walls in rivers like candle wax. I was aware of crying and calls for help. Heartbreaking cries, but I must have been in shock sufficiently to be unaffected. Then a door opened on the wall opposite, but further down the gallery to me. There came with it white light and vapour with people in it. They were unreal figures, oversized and salmon coloured, and so coated with vapour that it looked liked sugar.

The next thing I knew was of a boy raising his head up to speak to me. He said that he had been shouting to me for some time. He was shouting then, but it was as if he was whispering to me. I think he said that his name was Harry. We talked for some while. He was 16 . . . . we had both been entered for a scholarship. We talked about that mostly. Harry knew my grandmother would come for me. In 1940, wheelchairs were not very safe, and mine was known for its penchant for running away with me. I

could not handle the weight of the door, and Harry's back was broken. A beam had fallen on him. He had freed himself, and then crawled to where I was. Next we devised a plan. Harry would tip my wheelchair backwards and then push with his good side so as to force the exit door open. The plan worked well. I survived by that effort. Harry had said: "Do you know, if we survive this then we are going to be friends for life – aren't we?"

It became too hot to talk. Breathing became painful. Then I heard the man in the hallway say: "There she is! See! Her chair is sticking out of the exit doorway. Oh! It must be caught somewhere. It is not moving." Then they discovered Harry strapped to my chair. He acted like a brake, unfortunately. It must have been in that short time that he died. The last thing I heard him say was: "They are coming, Pat. Don't get excited and breathe too much, too deeply, like I just did. My! It hurts!"

The only girl from Central District Girls' School to survive the basement bombing, Audrey Hunt, will never forget November 6, 1940. She recalls:

I was 13, one of the oldest girls and about to leave Central. I was living in Northbrook Road at the time and had been attending the school since I was five. On that terrible day I remember the sirens sounding and suddenly we were all going down steps to a basement area. We had never been down there

before and we just followed the teachers. We had only been in there a few moments and then it all happened. I was in the corner of the room and had barely had time to sit down. I recall that a teacher was standing in front of me when suddenly there was a big thud. I looked up and saw the sky above. There was noise and screaming all around me. Just total chaos and confusion. Next, soldiers (I later learnt they were Canadians) appeared and formed a barrier to hold back a wall which was going to collapse. I must have been screaming to alert the rescuers because the "first aiders" came across to free me. A doctor then gave me an injection and I was taken to

87

South Hants Hospital. I remember I kept asking my parents where the other girls were and they told me they were in other wards. In fact only three others were alive at that point but they sadly passed away in hospital. They said it was shock that killed them which is probably true because my injuries were actually worse than theirs. In fact, I had acted as a shield because they had ended up underneath me. I had bad burns to my face and legs and I distinctly remember having saline baths which didn't hurt at all because the nerves in my legs were damaged. An army officer who came to look at me said he would just give it another weekend before deciding whether I needed plastic surgery. He came back on the Monday and saw that my legs had started to heal on their own so surgery wasn't necessary.

I was in hospital for four months in the end and afterwards I had awful nightmares about what happened down there. I often think about my friend Pamela Blackford who died. Her parents owned the Northumberland Hotel in Southampton and on that day she stayed behind at home to listen to the singer Leslie Hutchinson on the radio. Pamela ended up being late and she ran as fast as she could to get to the Art School. If she hadn't bothered she would be alive today. As for me, even now I wonder how on earth I was the only one to get out alive.

Thousands had been in the streets watching the aerial dogfight prior to the bombing raid. Now, as news about the Art School filtered through, the town was stunned. More horror lay in store. Britain was under aerial siege and it was Coventry's turn next. On November 14 more than 500 bombers dropped 500 tons of explosives and 900 flaming incendiaries during a relentless ten-hour bombardment. More than 300 Coventry citizens were killed. The Luftwaffe was now spreading the terror from London to provincial towns and cities.

Three days later, the first parachute mines floated down to Southampton killing fifteen people in the Manor Road area of Woolston and damaging more than 1,500 homes. However, it was the night of Saturday November 23, 1940, which heralded the beginning of the darkest week in Southampton's history. It was to be the town's first sustained night-time air raid and would be carried out by 120 bombers.

It started when a large number of incendiaries fell in the eastern part of

above: **A tram burnt out by incendiary in Bernard Street, Southampton, on November 23, 1940. The raid of November 23 was the first launched against the town along "classic" lines – namely flares to illuminate the target area, followed closely by incendiary showers and then high explosive bombs.**

Southampton. Then at 6.15pm a fearsome bombardment began. During the onslaught which followed, a firestorm of 4,000 incendiaries and 850 high explosive bombs – some fifty tons – descended upon the town according to official figures which now appear woefully conservative. The alert lasted until 7.34 the next morning, by which time seventy-seven people had lost their lives and more than 300 were injured. The water mains were ruined which meant many fires had to be left to burn themselves out; the Civic Centre was hit again; hundreds of shops were flattened; countless offices and businesses had vanished; thousands of homes were reduced to rubble; and thousands were homeless.

The fatalities that night included five firemen who were hit by high explosives while attempting to cope with the thousands of incendiaries which had preceded the bombing. Gwen Hughes, who had experienced the very first Southampton raid back in June, now believed husband Monty was among the dead firemen. She recalls:

Fires were blazing across the town that night and the sky was red. It was my husband's 32nd birthday and he and one other fireman were sent to a house opposite Palmerston Park to put out an incendiary. The rest of the crew were in the middle of the park with all the equipment because they thought that was the safest place to keep it. Then a bomb fell on the park and killed the five men standing there. The following morning, at about 3am, a policeman came into our shelter and said firemen had been killed. I thought my husband was one of them. I just couldn't believe he was alive and thought he had died on his birthday. Then, at 6am, he came in. I was so relieved and I just couldn't believe it was him standing there. He was covered in black and I couldn't recognize him at first.

Meanwhile, in the Chapel area that night, Vera and Bert Reynolds, the new landlords of the 19th century Garibaldi Arms public house, were entertaining twenty-four customers – including teenage English sailors who had just arrived in the town. The couple had only taken over the Garibaldi in Dock Street four weeks earlier and it was their first pub venture. It was an exciting new chapter for the Reynolds, even though one of their daughters, 14-year-old Olive,

right: **Firemen battle to control a blaze at the Smith Bradbeer store and neighbouring Picture House in Above Bar, November 23, 1940. After the attack, town Mayor, Cllr. William Lewis, said he had not seen "the slightest sign of panic" and praised the determination and high morale "which undoubtedly exists."**

had complained about moving from their home in Bitterne Park to a dangerous area so close to the Supermarine plant on the far bank of the Itchen. That evening, Olive, her two sisters and brother were upstairs in the pub while Eddie and Queenie Perry, a musical double act, entertained downstairs. Olive Rampton (nee Reynolds) recalls:

I had come home from working as a ledger clerk at Harrison's Dairies. Then my mother came upstairs to see us and said: "I think you had better get your coats on." I think she had had some sort of premonition that something was going to happen. My brother John (11) and my oldest sister Mary (16) then sat under one of the lift-up bar counters and I and my younger sister Dee (John's twin) sat under another one. At 8pm Jack Warner came on the radio and that was the last thing I remembered. I didn't hear the bomb. You never did. I then remembered Mary calling out to me and we were being helped out of the debris. I walked out of the crater that was left with my brother and sisters who had not been badly hurt. We sat down and then there was a commotion because they had noticed my left foot was hanging off. It was just being held on by a small piece of skin. I was carried to the Tagarts timber yard which had an emergency first aid post. I was in a shocked state and looked up at the sky and said: "Look at all the fireworks," unaware that the whole place was on fire. I was taken to another first aid centre at Chantry Hall before going to hospital.

I didn't recall anything then for a month due to unconsciousness and after about two months found out what had happened to my parents. I had been complaining to my uncle that my mum had not come to see me. I was really quite cross about it. My uncle got upset and went outside and a doctor came in, drew some blinds and told me my mum and dad had been killed in the pub bombing. I later learnt they were blown to bits and were put into one coffin. In fact twenty-six people died in that pub that night – us four children were the only survivors, probably because we had been beneath the bar counter. As for me, doctors decided to experiment and they saved my foot by performing one of the earliest skin grafts by taking skin from my thigh. I eventually came out of hospital in March 1941 and went to live with my aunt in St Mary's Road. In July an incendiary

destroyed that house and we were temporarily homeless before we moved to another house in Clovelly Road, just off St Mary's Road.

A strange thing happened in later life. In the 1960s, I happened to be working part time in Woolworth's and got talking to another employee called Mrs Marsh. It transpired she had been in one of those first aid centres and remembered helping me after the bomb blast. It was one of life's strange coincidences. Today, I can't stand war films and never watch Remembrance Day. I don't need any help remembering what happened.

The night of Saturday November 23 had introduced the town to the awesome capabilities of Goering's Luftwaffe. Seven days later, the bombers would come again and the consequences would eclipse the horror. It would be a "two night Blitz", not merely one. There would be a lot more incendiaries. There would be heavier bombs. There would be more deaths. The Luftwaffe would be closing in for the kill.

A beautiful pink sunset flushed over Southampton during the late afternoon of November 30, 1940. Shoppers looked to the heavens and admired God's handiwork unaware a man-made storm was on its way. It would be unsurpassed. It would be the big one. The terror started when a single bomb smashed into the pavement outside a restaurant called the Melbourne in the Lower High Street.

above: **The Reynolds family: Olive (front right) with, left to right, sisters Dorothy (Dee) and Mary, cousin Norah and brother John. The Garibaldi entertainer on that fateful night, Eddie Perry, had survived the Titanic disaster in April 1912. He was employed in the engine room but was safely inside a lifeboat when the giant liner slipped beneath the freezing Atlantic waters. After the November 23 raid, the Chapel district was in ruins. A journalist noted however: "No sooner had the bombing ceased than out of these broken and shattered houses emerged housewives, who, with broom in hand, proceeded to sweep clean their doorsteps."**

CHAPTER 6

"Gloria's all right but I think Anthony is finished"

The Blitz of Southampton, November 30 and December 1, 1940

THE rubble had entombed them. Gwen Hughes couldn't move. Dirt caked her mouth. Shock paralysed her brain. They had been buried alive. Then the noises. Explosions. Cries. Agonising screeches from the depths of the subterranean cave. Next a familiar voice.

"Mummy, Mummy. Are you all right, Mummy?" Gwen's five-year-old daughter Gloria was calling. She had been sitting close to her mother before the darkness, the noise, the horror. The little girl's two-and-a-half-year–old brother, Anthony, had also been nearby. Where was everyone now? Where was Mum?

Gwen had managed to cover her son's head with one hand and a wooden ledge above the children held back tons of masonry which now threatened to crush them. Then another familiar voice from outside the bombed air raid shelter. It was her husband, Monty, a fireman. "Gwen, Gwen!" he shouted from somewhere above.

"My family is down there! MY FAMILY IS DOWN THERE!" he was now shouting. Gwen couldn't speak. She heard another man reply. "It's no good going down there, mate, they are all finished." Mrs Hughes, who had experienced the first raid on Southampton five months earlier, recalls:

On Saturday November 30 my father told me he had to go out and had asked if I would go and look after the family restaurant, The Melbourne, which

left: Five-year-old Gloria and two-year-old Anthony Hughes. Together with their mother Gwen, they were buried alive when the Melbourne Restaurant shelter was bombed.

was also a hotel. The Melbourne was situated at the bottom of the High Street in Southampton. It was a wonderful twelve-bedroom place with a marvellous spiral staircase. It was first opened as a restaurant by my grandfather and my dad had taken it over in 1919. It was home from home to all the seamen and there was always a roaring fire inside. They loved going there. At about five minutes to 6pm on the night of November 30, the flares, which the Germans used to light up targets for bombing, started to fall. The sirens also started and then all hell broke loose. The cellar of the restaurant — which consisted of three chambers — was used as a public shelter and I went down there with my children and put on their blue "Siren Suits", which were little warm jumpsuits with hoods. Inside one of the shelters my husband had fitted a wooden shelf inside a narrow stone arch which was about 18 inches (46 cms) wide. It was just right for the children to fit under during raids to give them added protection. My two went under the ledge and I stood in front of them.

Then the bombs came. The first bomb — one I later discovered was the first one of the entire raid — landed on the pavement at the front of the double-fronted restaurant, bursting a water main. At the time I had just got in the shelter and was asking a man called Pat Powell for a light for my cigarette. Mr Powell was offering me the light and just then the second bomb landed. The blast came through the wall and into the back of him. I was standing right in front of Mr Powell and he took the full impact. Another couple were hit too at that moment. The Mays, who had a sweet shop in the High Street, had just returned from Bristol where they had gone to escape the Southampton bombing. The wife had just asked her husband: "Why, oh why have we come back?" He had replied: "The business, my dear, the business," and it was then that the wall came in. He took the blast in the back of the head and I later learnt that it was severed. His wife was killed too and their 13-year-old daughter, Sheila, who had celebrated her birthday the day before. Next the whole restaurant — four storeys — caved in on top of the shelter. I had my hand on Anthony's head and reached for Gloria too as tons of stuff fell down. I thought: "This is it. We are finished." But, to my amazement, I knew I was alive. I could still think and dribble the dirt out of my mouth. I must have eventually said something too because my husband knew I was alive down there. It was terrible to hear my husband calling outside.

The water from the burst water main was seeping through the rubble by now and at one point it was up to my chest. I later realised the flood had drowned my lovely dogs, Pronto and Peggy, and her eight puppies which she had had in the previous week. They all drowned. My husband, who had earlier been on the roof of The Melbourne clearing off incendiaries, was by now working with others to dig me out. My husband said to someone: "What are we going to do if we can't get them out?" Then there was talk of shooting me to put me out of the misery of drowning. I was terrified but after five hours they managed to lift me out. I remember asking Monty about the children and he said: "Gloria's all right but I think Anthony is finished." I fainted at that point but was told later he had made it even though he

left: Gloria and Anthony's mother, Gwen Hughes pictured while courting husband-to-be Monty.

was traumatised.

When I was taken out of the shelter, it felt as if I had been reborn but even then it wasn't over. When I was being taken down the street a bomb exploded 50 yards (45 metres) behind me as well. We carried on and I remember the scenes to this day. The entire High Street was a huge wall of fire and flames. That's the only way I can describe it. I was taken to hospital but amazingly I wasn't really physically hurt except for my leg where a pick used to dig me out had struck me. The hand I used to protect my son's head was also broken and I couldn't hold a cup for fifteen weeks. But that hand saved Anthony. Thankfully, Gloria was safe, too. But I will never forget the screams I heard that night. In fact, I

left: Gloria and Anthony's father, Monty, who helped pull his children from the rubble.

couldn't get them out of my head for years and years after. I kept hearing their exact screams as if it was happening again and again and again."

Twenty-eight people had been in the shelter. Gwen and her two children were the only survivors. However many, many more lost their lives during a battering which lasted six hours – and which had a repeat performance the following night, Sunday December 1. A total of 137 were to die that weekend and 471 were injured. Hitler's Luftwaffe had finally unleashed the sickening horror of the Blitzkrieg upon Southampton.

Geoffrey O'Connor, then chief reporter of the Southern Daily Echo, gave the paper an eyewitness account of the moments that preceded the terror that weekend: "Saturday, November 30, 1940, had darkened into a cold, crisp night when the air raid sirens moaned in dismal chorus. Scarcely had the wailing faded when the sky above Southampton began to change colour. Between the blacked-out town and the German raiders, droning high at first, then daringly low, there glided down, slowly, ominously and ever brighter, the parachute flares that picked out the Luftwaffe's target for the night. Soon the flares were countless. They shed a merciless glare on a town that was within the next six hours to rock and tremble and become a blazing mass…"

Bernard Knowles, in an account he later published in "Southampton: The English Gateway", takes up the description with this graphic, almost poetic recollection: "The turmoil was indescribable. Endless cascades of incendiaries were interspersed with torrents of high explosive bombs. Even the most savage convulsion of nature could convey no idea of the universal uproar and clamour. Every possible form of terror was present. Every second or two the town was shaken to its foundations. The air was a whirling frenzy; hot blasts swept the streets; the town was quickly becoming a sea of flame from which, in regular and horrible sequence, rose cascades of flying debris, red and yellow vapour, and swirling columns of smoke….a terrifying

situation developed. Crump followed crump; explosion followed explosion; the earth gaped. Jets of fire, smoke and debris flew upwards like the spouting of giant whales. The walls of huge buildings, cracked at their bases, at first oscillated, then bowed to one another like grave old courtiers, and finally prostrated themselves with a frightful crash … hour after hour, with high explosives dropping like rain, an army of steel-helmeted firemen, armed with hose and axe, wrestled like Titans with the flames. Striking here, hacking there, grand amidst the holocaust, nearly a thousand fire-fighters strode the blazing ruins."

Hitler's objective was clear – he had ordered the total annihilation of the town. One hundred and twenty Luftwaffe aircraft attacked on each night of that bloody weekend. Official figures, which historians believe are again grossly conservative, state that 105 tons of bombs fell upon buildings, shelters, homes and people. The bombers unloaded fewer explosives that weekend than on the previous Saturday (November 23) – 800 compared to 850. However, they were double the weight. Some 9,000 incendiaries accompanied the bombs ensuring 670 separate fires were also caused. The resulting fireball could be seen in France – and by the German crews when they returned on Sunday night. Fires, in fact, caused greater damage than explosions and the historic and commercial centre was largely gutted. The townscape changed forever and had, according to Knowles, "become a smouldering catacomb, a reeking mass of calcinated brick and blackened stone. It was as though the town had been the victim of a savage and brutal assassination."

Some 1,169 properties were wrecked and more than 4,500 damaged. Landmark premises like Pirelli's, Ordnance Survey and the Rank Flour Mill in the New Docks were also partially demolished. The famous Edwin Jones store received a direct hit and was destroyed as was the Plummer Roddis premises, Gabriel Wade's timber yard and the General Motors Factory. Cinemas, theatres and pubs – the great focal points for recharging

left: The Plummer Roddis store before the raid.

below: The Plummer Roddis premises in Above Bar: Gutted after the weekend raid of November 30/December 1, 1940.

morale – were also reduced to twisted metal and heaps of smoking rubble. The Echo office was gutted too. The staff immediately moved to the sister paper in Bournemouth to complete Monday's edition which duly appeared with the full story of the raid. Fourteen main churches – including the "mother" church of St Mary, St Luke's, Holy Rood, St James', Above Bar Congregational and the Baptist Church in Portland Street – were among the places of worship lost. The Civic Centre was also so badly smashed that temporary headquarters were established in the Polygon Hotel.

Those in the front line faced a desperate situation. The town's fire service was reinforced by 2,000 men and 160 vehicles from around the country, with crews arriving from Nottingham, Ipswich and Peterborough. Yet the firestorm was getting completely out of hand. Flames had engulfed the telephone exchange and

then fire broke out in the nurses' block at the Royal South Hants Hospital. Seventy-eight patients had to be quickly evacuated and moved to other hospitals.

Fifteen -year -old cinema projectionist Sam Cooper had a bird's-eye view of the Saturday night raid and vividly remembers the aftermath. He recalls:

I watched everything from my crow's nest – the 100ft roof of the Regal Cinema in Above Bar. The cinema's projection room was at the top of the building and a small iron ladder on the outside wall led to the actual roof itself. We watched it all go on from up there. In the cinema that night I and another young projectionist were left to run the film. It was Bob Hope in The Ghost Breakers. We always had this thing that the show must go on and so we just carried on regardless, despite what was happening outside. The building then started shaking when the bombs dropped. Then a couple of incendiaries dropped on the roof and I and the other young lad went up there and knocked them off into the street

left: Inside the composing room of the Southern Daily Echo after the "Blitz Weekend".

below. I went back down into the cinema and put the projector on variable speed to hurry it up, which was prohibited. I remember one scene where a zombie was chasing Bob Hope. He suddenly went along like Linford Christie! People were still watching not realising the cinema had an asbestos roof. One incendiary even came down by the organ pit in the front stalls. It did not go off but people threw themselves under their seats. Still the film went on but people were starting to get concerned. We only had about fifty people in there and after the film and National Anthem, Roy (the cinema doorman) led them across to the shelters in the parks. Our own cinema basement had a large crowd inside already. The scene in *Above Bar* was awful. I remember the *Palace Theatre* was rubble and the *Echo* was on fire. Scullards, a bar, was on fire too and the landlady told us to take what we wanted. Four airmen walked in and they pulled up a barrel from the cellar. They disappeared into the flames, rolling the barrel along the road. There was also a smell of frying bacon – a grocery called Pinks used to dress its windows with sides of bacon and it was frying. I can't remember seeing any police, firemen or anyone. It was just one massive fire.

The late Arthur Gledhill, who was manager of the Clarence pub in the High Street, was working as an auxiliary fireman that night. He was blown against a wall and almost buried beneath rubble when a bomb fell killing a colleague. Mr Gledhill later wrote vividly of other experiences that night:

. . . .Several incendiaries were burning on the opposite pavement. I crossed the road and kicked them into the gutter. Whilst thus occupied, I heard someone calling: "Help, help! I can't see." I returned to see one of our men floundering about amongst the debris that had fallen into a bomb crater. I called to him and as he turned in the direction of my voice, I was able to grasp his hand and pull him out. The blast had caught him full in the face, blinding him. I cleared a space and got him to lie down, pillowing his head on his service respirator as some ARP men arrived and they took over and an ambulance was sent for. I got under a fallen ramp and released another of our men who had become partially buried and, while doing so, another bomb exploded across the road and blew me into the wall again. Shortly after this the ambulance arrived. I had to admire the young woman driver, she was as cool as a cucumber, backing up the ambulance amongst the debris and waiting while the injured and one body were put on board. I sat in the back between the stretchers. All this time there was the noise of HE (high explosives) falling and exploding, guns firing and the roar of the fires of burning buildings. Shrapnel was falling like hail – such was the situation when we set off for hospital . . .

right below: **Above Bar before the war showing Cinenews which opened in 1937 (to become the Classic Cinema in 1938) and the Picture House to the left. The building with the shop front blinds over the pavement is Smith Bradbeer.**

right above: **The same view after the Blitz of November 30/ December 1, 1940. The bombed Classic Cinema in Above Bar had opened in 1938 when the first film was "Keep Your Seats Please" with George Formby. To celebrate the occasion milk shakes were free in the café. During the "Blitz Weekend", customers left the cinema as incendiaries rained down. Some thought they saw bodies as they fled but the torsos were in fact dummies from the nearby Burton's clothes store. The Picture House.**

above: **Young Sam Cooper**, the Regal Cinema projectionist.

to the left of the Classic, was probably the most luxurious cinema Southampton has had. It opened on May 24, 1920 with a programme about Ernest Shackleton's Antarctic Expedition and a Mary Pickford film. "Wagons Westward" was the last film shown before it was destroyed on the night of November 30, 1940. A police officer appeared on the stage during the screening and ordered all the customers to leave in an orderly fashion starting with the front row. The damaged Classic reopened showing well-known films and in the 1970s a small screen built above the foyer served the little Tatler private cinema which specialised in "adult" films. Both closed in 1978. The Picture House was never rebuilt.

Mr Gledhill began to wonder if his wife Hilda, six-year-old daughter Veronica and four-year-old son Michael had survived the raid. The next day he left the Borough General Hospital and made his way back to the Clarence pub to find out. He wrote:

Arriving at Holy Rood, the fine old church was just a shell, its spire lay across the road, other buildings lay in ruins. I looked and saw that what was left of the Clarence (the rear had been wrecked in September, see page 53) *was still standing and, to my utmost joy, found my wife and children safe.*

His loved ones had their own stories to tell from the harrowing previous night. Mr Michael Gledhill recalls:

I was just six weeks short of my fifth birthday that evening. The sirens were sounding and my mum

there was another shelter. My mum and I thought the policeman was crying and I asked him why. The policeman replied that he wasn't crying – he was sweating in the intense heat and from the exertion of carrying me on his back. We then went into the vault of St Michael's Church where we stayed until the all-clear in the morning.

When Mum took us home there was devastation everywhere. In French Street at the back of Mowat's the fishmongers we saw just one fireman yet there seemed to be lots of hoses. My mum gave him a swig of brandy from a hip flask she carried with her. Our side of the High Street had got the worst of it but our pub was still standing. Macfisheries next door had gone, however, while Gosney's the tobacconists had survived. Then a whole lot of shops all the way up to Castle Lane were gone too. Our dog Tiny had been killed but my dad was at least relieved to find the money was still in the tills at the Clarence. We moved out to Redbridge until the Clarence was made habitable again. When we got back, my pals and I had the biggest adventure playground of all. We played in all the bombed crater sites.

For young entertainer Brenda Pritchett (nee Logie), that Saturday night of November 30 was meant to have been rather special. She recalls:

It was a big night because it was going to be the first time I was allowed to go to a grown-up dance and I had a date. I was going with a boy that I knew and also a girlfriend of mine who came from Totton. We had just got into the Guildhall when the raid started. The bombs dropped right by the side of the Guildhall and all the glass in the foyer was shattered. It fell on us as we stood there. Everyone was told to leave the place and outside it was really getting bad. There was lots of noise and fire everywhere. The boy and I could have got back home because we lived in Bassett. However, my friend lived in Totton and the public transport system stopped when the raid began so she had no way of getting home. We stayed with her and then a group of soldiers came along. We decided it would be safer to stay with them and look for a shelter.

As we walked, all the shops along the High Street started catching fire. It was like Dante's Inferno. The soldiers ended up giving us two girls their helmets and made sure we walked between them down the road. When we got to Ogle Road, a little man seemed to come out of the ground and asked if we wanted to get into his half-finished shelter. We went down the ladder and listened to all the din from down there. Then I suddenly thought to myself – and this sounds

wakened me and my six-year-old sister Veronica and put mackintoshes over our pyjamas before taking us out of the Clarence pub and to the air raid shelter. Our shelter was on the opposite side of the High Street not far from Holy Rood church. I remember the bunks and blankets in there but after a while we were told we would have to move because of the incendiary bombs. We were taken to another cellar further along the High Street but were then told to move yet again. When we came up to street level, I remember the scene was as bright as day with the light from the burning buildings. Holy Rood Church was ablaze from end to end, the spire was gone, the roof was gone, and also all the windows. It was just a big inferno. The tower which once supported the spire was now like a Roman candle with masses of sparks coming from the top. The flames shot at least 30 feet (9 metres) into the air. My mum was helping my sister so a policeman carried me on his back up St Michael's Street to St Michael's Square where

above: **Aftermath in St Mary's church. Valuable relics – including seventeenth century registers – were saved but a rare 400-year-old picture was lost. The church was the fifth that had stood on the site. It was now a black shell but its spire rose triumphantly into the winter sky.**

left: **The Clarence, managed by Arthur Gledhill (inset).**

top: **Young Michael Gledhill.**

above: **Michael's sister Veronica. Both children were taken by their mother Hilda to three different shelters on the night of Saturday November 30 in order to avoid the firestorm.**

the air but he landed alive in a flowerbed.

The Echo praised the actions of ambulance drivers when its edition came out on Monday: "At the height of the raid, when the bombs were falling from waves of raiders, they drove through the streets with the courage of front line troops. Here is the experience of one young girl which was typical of many. A bomb fell not far from her ambulance as she was driving to an incident and it blew her vehicle up on to the pavement. Jumping from the driver's seat to find out the damage, she saw three men lying in the road badly injured. Unaided, she lifted them one by one into her ambulance and drove them to hospital."

However, despite such uplifting stories, there was no disguising the scale of the catastrophe. The Echo, its Monday front page headlined "Germans Savage Southampton", reported: "Many Southampton people are demanding the compulsory evacuation of women and children. The Bishop of Winchester, Dr Cyril Garbett, who spent two days visiting the bombed areas, told a Press representative he found conditions 'really serious'. There was a great need to get away many old and infirm people and as many children as possible … thousands of people are without homes and hundreds have been rendered unemployed … the business office district was again the main objective, but some areas in the suburbs were left in ruins. In one road not a house escaped some damage."

The shelters had not escaped either when the bombs rained down. In fact, ninety-six of the 137 who died that weekend were killed as they cowered in shelters. Descending bombs simply ripped through the roofs. Jean Thorn, the little evacuee who had run away from her Christchurch billet, was inside the family Anderson shelter in Millbrook listening to the thunderous bedlam outside. She recalls:

Suddenly there was a huge blast and it obliterated our family home in Victory Road and sent a shower

really silly now — I had better do something with my hair or it would be a mess for the show I was doing the next day. Boys in those days always wore black coats and white scarves if they were going to a formal dance and I asked the chap I was with if I could have his scarf. Next, I got my curlers out. I had them with me because I was due to stay at my singing teacher's house that night before doing the show the next day. I then put my long hair up in the curlers and tied the boy's scarf round my head in a turban. That, I'm afraid, was the most important thing to a young teenager even if the Blitz was happening. When we came out you could have stolen anything. All the stuff was hanging out of the shops. But, you know, I didn't see anyone take anything at all. Then little groups started forming and lifts home were organised.

That weekend, amid the searing terror and sickening carnage, there were acts of extraordinary bravery. A porter who saw an incendiary land on a hospital roof leapt 7 feet (2.1m) from a nearby building to reach it. He used his bare hands to scoop off the bomb into the street below. As his burnt hands were bandaged, a bomb blew him high into

of masonry on top of our garden Anderson shelter. There was an eerie silence and then my dad said: "Don't panic, but I think we have been buried alive," which wasn't very reassuring. I can also remember the reek of garden herbs mingling with the smell of sulphur and cordite from the bombs. I also recall the moment when I realised one of my sisters, Dorrie, was missing. The candle was blown out so it was pitch black inside the shelter. But we eventually found an arm sticking out from a pile of rubble and we pulled her out. She was unconscious but OK. Then a neighbour located us and managed to help us all out within half-an-hour.

It was the second time we had been bombed out of a house in Victory Road. A bomb had once hit the top of our shelter at our old house a few doors up the road and slid down the side without exploding. It felt as if we had been hit by a 100-pound hammer. We had to move to another house in Victory Road just in case it suddenly went up. It was therefore an amazing coincidence when our old house was hit once again during the Blitz night and the blast damaged the house we had moved into. It was the explosion at the old place which caused us to be buried in the shelter at the new one! The night before that big Saturday raid, we had gone to the shelter again. My dad had tried to get my Aunty Topsy to go too but she collapsed and died in her armchair. I still remember her false teeth flying out and clattering across the

lino. I was transfixed in horror. We all went to live in Millbrook Road after the terrible "Blitz Weekend".

Ten-year-old Brian Simpson was also lucky to survive the "Blitz Weekend" inside the family shelter. Mr Simpson recalls:

On the Sunday night, December 1, I was in our Anderson shelter in Oaktree Road, Bitterne Park. We had gone through our usual shelter routine: we had our Cocoa made with condensed milk and then headed for the Anderson with Mum, Dad, my 16-year-old brother and 13-year-old sister. I went to bed fully dressed as usual apart from my trousers and shoes and waited to see what the night held in store. Incidentally, I was to spend 400 nights in that shelter bed which consisted of a wooden board and a blanket folded over three times on top to act as a mattress. When that big raid started, the anti-aircraft guns in Allington Lane started up. They were as noisy as the bombs and the whole place started rattling and vibrating. Mud, water and muck started to come through the roof of the shelter where the curved metal plates joined. There was a massive bang when one bomb landed in Manor Farm Road and the blast came over us blowing the front door of our house half-way up the stairs. The ARP man for the area came round and told us he had been round to

above: **The medieval Holy Rood Church: before and after the main "Blitz Weekend".**

above: **Jean Thorn, the runaway evacuee, who escaped death once back home in Millbrook.**

100

Manor Farm Road and shone his torch in a shelter. Four people — two adults and two children — were sat in there and looked completely normal. But the bomb blast had sucked the air out of the shelter and they were in fact dead even though their bodies were unmarked.

In the morning we had our usual porridge for breakfast and then ripped lino off the floor of our house to put over the smashed windows. Then another delayed action bomb — one deliberately dropped to go up later — exploded, which gave us a hell of a shock. We heard a lady shout: "Help!" and people went to get her out from beneath the rubble. Wood and bricks were passed to me and then someone said: "Get a rope." I went to get the washing line and they used it to pull the woman out. I remember she was holding a baby girl close to her and they were both all right. I went home and the first thing Mum said was: "Where's our washing line?"

Some of the most tragic incidents occurred in the public shelters that tragic weekend of November 30/December 1. One shelter in Houndwell Park received a direct hit. Young Brian Simpson was told by his father, a Borough Engineer's shelter inspector, what happened. Mr Simpson recalls:

The Houndwell Park shelter was used by the people from St Mary's who didn't have gardens. I remember when it was hit and Dad said around fifty people were killed inside. Shelters were blast-proof but they were not bomb-proof. That night those people were blown to pieces in there and people were going around afterwards with baskets trying to pick up bits of bodies and clear up the mess. (Another eyewitness recalled seeing a shocked ARP man emerging from the scene holding just a severed hand.) Dad said they didn't know exactly how many were down there and the rescuers didn't want to go back in because it was just so awful. There was basically nothing left to take out. No-one was alive and they concreted the place over in the end.

A week later I went with Mum to buy a knife from a shop in Bernard Street for Christmas but when we got there the place had gone. In fact nearly all the street was gone. There was still smoke everywhere and my eyes watered. To this day I don't know whether I was crying or whether the smoke brought tears to my eyes. As we came back home past Houndwell Park I remember seeing bits of clothing that had been blown into the trees by the bomb. You couldn't help but look up and for months and months there was half a jacket hanging from a branch. Gradually it started to get tatty and weathered.

In the wind the sleeve almost waved at you.

left: Family at war: (left to right): Dorothy Kelly (nee Dinsdale), far left, supports cousin Barbara Godwin. Dorothy's Aunt Nellie (holding blankets) follows together with Grandmother Sarah Fenton (clutching bag in centre) and Uncle William (holding briefcases in foreground). Dorothy's mum, Amy Pope, follows at the rear of the group with Dorothy's half-sister, Pamela.

Southampton, the great port town that had seen Henry V's forces leave for Agincourt and the Great War troops depart for the trenches, had been battered into ruins. There was no gas, no telephones, precious little water and not much electricity. Crowds gathered around lists pinned outside the police station. They recorded the dead. Southampton was a town deep in shock.

On December 1, 1940, fifteen out of twenty-one emergency centres opened up in the town and hundreds of homeless citizens flocked to them. A new evacuation was soon organised. Before dusk fell, nearly 700 had been evacuated to Chandler's Ford and other places further afield.

The next day, December 2, a further 4,000 people left. An eyewitness wrote: "The roads leading out of the port were crowded with homeless families bound for the comparative safety of seaside and country." Hundreds, added the observer, simply walked, pushed prams laden with household goods and wheeled bicycles supporting mattresses.

During the morning, vans equipped with loudspeakers toured the town advertising the evacuation of men and women and urging restraint with water and electricity usage. Large numbers now left and whole streets became deserted.

That day, one particular family was photographed walking through the scorched ruins on their way to the countryside. Dorothy Kelly (nee Dinsdale) recalls:

I was 19 years old at the time of that dreadful raid on Sunday December 1 and will never forget it. I was in the surface shelter opposite our home in Birmingham Street with my mum Amy and Aunty Nellie. My 15-year-old cousin Barbara Godwin was there too and she was in a terrible state. She had pleurisy brought on by the terrible vibration of the explosions which had damaged her lungs and made her very congested and weak. In the morning we crossed over to our house opposite and picked up some possessions to take with us to King's Somborne where my cousins Patricia and Marie were waiting. Then we walked to the bus stop in Pound Tree Road and that's when the picture (see above) was taken. In the photograph I'm carrying a big box. That was full of shoes and stockings because I didn't want to leave them behind in Southampton. We didn't know when we were coming back. Poor Barbara could hardly breathe as we made our way down Above Bar and that's why she held on to my arm. There were flames everywhere and complete devastation. We just had to get out of there. We were actually stopped at one point by firemen who were diverting people but they

above: Brian Simpson, who had a lucky escape in the family Anderson shelter in Bitterne Park.

right: **King George VI inspects rescue and emergency teams at the Civic Centre with Mayor William Lewis (left) and Dr Maurice Williams (Medical Officer of Health), right.**

below: **King George VI (centre of leading group) accompanied by Mayor William Lewis inspects Above Bar. The bombed out Southern Daily Echo offices are to his right. The wintry streets echoed to cheers and cries of "God Save the King" as the tour progressed.**

left: Asleep in Brickwoods Brewery underground shelter in Bedford Place, Southampton. Little Margaret Green, aged eight, posed for this shot for a Daily Echo photographer in December 1940. Margaret recalls: "I was in the shelter with around eight children and we had a party after the picture was taken." After the "Blitz Weekend" of November 30, a rousing Daily Echo editorial commented: "It would be a distortion of the truth not to admit that these two raids left Sotonians shaken physically and mentally. But it must be recorded too, that the Luftwaffe's viciousness had not broken the spirit of the people... everywhere one found a new spirit of helpfulness; everywhere was neighbourliness at its best." The old custom of seeing in the New Year at Holy Rood Church continued too. Forty people stood amid the rubble to sing "Auld Lang Syne".

realised Barbara was unwell and they let us through. Barbara pulled through and we all got to King's Somborne in the end.

Three days after the family left, King George VI, accompanied by the Minister of Home Security, Herbert Morrison, arrived to see the ruined town for himself. They were met by Southampton Mayor William Lewis, who had that day praised the "magnificent spirit which the townspeople had shown in affliction". By the Civic Centre, the King inspected police, rescue squads and fire and ambulance teams – unaware that an unexploded bomb lay nearby in the Forum Cinema. The auxiliary fireman Arthur Gledhill, manager of the Clarence pub, was in the front row as the King approached. He later wrote:

... As I still had my bandages, His Majesty stopped in front of me. But with what he had seen, I think he was too choked to speak and, with a look full of sympathy, passed on down the line.

Stony-faced, the King then walked down Above Bar and inspected the aftermath of Blitzkrieg as troops cleared the debris around him. He smiled occasionally. He even raised his hat to passers-by. Yet there was not, in truth, a great deal he could say. Nazi bombing during two consecutive weekends in November had killed at least 214 people in the town. Others were to commit suicide in the days that followed. These were the facts of the matter. This was the scale of the tragedy. The people of Southampton were not to know that this was very worst that Goering could offer. They were not to know that the end would eventually be in sight. Equally, they could never imagine that one of the hated bombers was about to crash in the town.

CHAPTER 7

A bomber hit our house, Janet

Nazis fall to earth and Blitz closedown, 1941 and 1942

THE little girl's Teddy bear was found amid the rubble, his face beaming curiously from the fallen masonry. His golden beige fur was dirty but "Ted's" little pink coat was keeping him warm. Two-year-old Janet Groves dusted him down, gave him a cuddle, and surveyed what remained of her home, 19 Padwell Road, Southampton. There was nothing. Thankfully Janet, and her mother Freda, had been spending nights with a family in Testwood, Totton, and returned to Padwell Road only in the mornings. Now mother and daughter were sifting through the debris in a vain bid to rescue possessions. Two orange vases were the only other items they could find.

Stepping outside the shell of their home, they were shocked to see that a bizarre lunar landscape had replaced what had once been their road. They saw that Number 12, the unoccupied, rambling home belonging to Kate and Fred Mortlock, had been reduced to a smouldering heap of bricks. Mr Mortlock had taken his wife and her sister to Exeter to escape the bombing. What a shock awaited them on their return. More than a decade of family memories completely wiped out. A package containing three large Bibles and a picture of an angel hanging on the one remaining wall was all that could be salvaged from the Mortlocks' home.

Nine other homes nearby were also badly damaged but, miraculously, no-

one had been killed. Little Janet Groves' father, Bert, then spotted a strange piece of metal inscribed with a four-digit code. Unknown to the family, he held the one clue to what had caused the devastation in Padwell Road on the night of April 15, 1941. That small piece of metal was the manufacturer's number plate from a German Heinkel He 111 bomber which had been hurtling homewards through the inky darkness above Southampton on that fateful evening.

left: **Janet Groves in the garden at 19 Padwell Road, Southampton.**

left: The remnants of the downed Heinkel bomber lying at the Oxford Road-Padwell Road junction in Southampton.

Cocooned inside the Heinkel, the bomber crew could not see the tragic legacy of the ferocious bombing campaign which had been inflicted on the town below. However, someone could see them. As they headed for home, the pilot was unaware of a RAF Beaufighter just 90 metres behind it. The hands clasped on the Beaufighter throttle and the keen eyes penetrating the black void belonged to Squadron Leader John "Cats Eyes" Cunningham. Alongside him was his radar operator, Sergeant Cecil Rawnsley. The kill was moments way.

Inside the Heinkel bomber, 25-year-old pilot Gunther von Seidlitz was anxious to get his aircraft back to base in occupied France. Von Seidlitz was a highly experienced bomber pilot who had risen to the rank of Oberleutnant – the equivalent of a RAF Flying Officer. To his right sat Feldwebel (Sergeant) Franz

Hummer, aged 26, who was the observer and also responsible for navigation, bomb aiming and the machine-gun in the nose cone. Behind them sat wireless operator and dorsal gunner, Unteroffizier (Corporal) Herbert Sauer and ventral gunner and flight engineer, Unteroffizier Horst Rosenberg, both aged 21.

Their Heinkel had set off that evening from the Villacoublay airfield in France with a full bomb load to drop on Liverpool. Fifty other German bombers had accompanied the Heinkel over the English Channel on its deadly mission. Merseyside had been pounded and large fires now raged in the docks. Von Seidlitz's bomber had been unable to locate the target area and turned for France with its bomb load still on board. Now the hunter was about to be hunted.

Squadron Leader Cunningham had first seen searchlights sweeping the sky near Marlborough and felt this might indicate the position of a homeward-bound bomber. He went to investigate and Sergeant Rawnsley soon made radar contact. The doomed Heinkel was approaching the South Coast slightly to the west of Southampton when "Cats Eyes" unleashed his cannons. Seconds later, the German bomber banked to the left with both Daimler-Benz engines on fire. It began to plummet towards Southampton at terrifying speed.

Aboard the stricken aircraft, pilot von Seidlitz ordered Hummer to jettison the bomb load. Eight bombs landed north east of Marchwood. They did not explode because von Seidlitz, intending to take the bombs home, probably disconnected the fuses to make the journey safer. By now, the scramble to get out of the Heinkel had begun. All four jumped out, leaving the fireball to fall to earth. It crashed, in a deafening crescendo of noise, in Padwell Road. The downed

right: RAF personnel carry the coffins containing von Seidlitz and Hummer at South Stoneham Cemetery on Friday April 18, 1941.

Heinkel was the first – and believed to be the only – enemy aircraft known to have crashed within the town limits.

High above the street, "Cats Eyes" Cunningham and radar operator Rawnsley watched in horror as the crash site glowed red and orange below. Yet their fears of huge casualties were unwarranted – no-one had been killed and the damage was relatively minimal and restricted. A Southern Daily Echo

reporter witnessed the whole incident and recalled: "I heard three planes go over. This was followed immediately by a terrific roar of engines as the machine dived to its doom. A sheet of flame shot up when the plane hit the ground. It burnt fiercely for a few minutes and then, with a vivid flash as though incendiaries had gone off, the fire died out. The wreckage of the house which was demolished caught fire and blazing fuel

right: **Horst Rosenberg's widow, Dr. Annemarie Rosenberg.**

spread a fiery trail over the road."

Nearby, Mrs G T Light and her three teenage children were in their garden shelter when the bomber crashed, damaging their home. Her husband returned from work to be confronted by devastation. He told the Echo reporter: "We had only been in the house five weeks. We moved from the lower part of the town because we thought it would be safer."

Meanwhile, as the drama unfolded in Padwell Road, the four German crewmen were falling through the night sky. Oberleutnant von Seidlitz and his observer, Feldwebel Hummer, may well have been clutching the same parachute when they hurled themselves out of the escape hatch in the side of the Heinkel fuselage. When the parachute was found caught on a crane jib in the Northam yard of Pollock and Brown, the dead body of von Seidlitz hung in the harness. Close by lay the body of Hummer with no sign of the means by which he descended. Both men were buried with full military honours on Friday April 18, 1941, at South Stoneham Cemetery. The two coffins, each covered with a German flag and borne on the shoulders of six Royal Air Force personnel, were placed in a single grave before a wreath of pink carnations and tulips was placed on top

by a RAF sergeant. A central war cemetery for German war dead was later opened twenty miles north of Birmingham on Cannock Chase and it was there that the remains of the two crewmen found their final resting place.

A quarter of a mile from where von Seidlitz and Hummer met their deaths in the Northam scrapyard, fellow crewman Unteroffizier Herbert Sauer hit a front garden brick wall, breaking one or both his legs. Mrs J A Rose rushed out of her house and found him screaming for help, his parachute entangled in a nearby tree. "He looked very young and was unarmed," said Mrs Rose. "He could speak no English but was very grateful for what we did." Her husband and two sons removed the young man's parachute harness and made him comfortable until an ambulance arrived. He was then taken to the Royal South Hants Hospital, which was just a short distance away. Sauer was to spend the rest of the conflict as a prisoner-of-war.

The final member of the crew, Unteroffizier Horst Rosenberg, had meanwhile crashed into the roof of a stationary guard's van in the Mount Pleasant marshalling yard. He was unhurt apart from a cut lip and, after freeing himself from his parachute, he started to walk down the railway track. A shunter's hut loomed ahead and Rosenberg, dressed in full Luftwaffe issue flying uniform, stepped inside and gave himself up to a stunned inspector, Mr Alfred Frewin. Mr Frewin asked him to surrender his pistol and Rosenberg obliged.

The German airman, who spoke only a little English, was then treated to a cup of tea and a cigarette while they waited for the police to arrive. Rosenberg was taken to Portswood police station for the night before beginning life as a prisoner-of-war.

Both surviving crewmen returned to Germany after the war. Herbert Sauer died in July 1996, Horst Rosenberg in July 1983 at the age of 63 following a heart attack. Rosenberg's widow Annemarie is today a doctor living in Tirol, Austria, close to their youngest daughter. She recalls:

Horst spent a year as an English PoW before being sent to Canada. He then returned to England. When he was a prisoner, he was sent many books through the Red Cross including medical ones. The medical profession was the one he decided to join when he eventually returned to his parents in Leipzig – which was then in East Germany – in 1947. He went on to study medicine and that's how we met each other in 1949, because I was also studying medicine in Leipzig. We married after some years and Horst became a specialist in surgery. Horst often said how moved he was by the British funeral of the two German crewmen who died in the crash. He thought it was so touching, dignified and respectful. He was amazed by that. I took the urn of Horst with me to Austria when I moved there in 1989. Now I can always care for his grave. As for the war, it is so important that everyone still remembers all the young people who gave their lives. They must never be forgotten. Never.

The little Southampton girl who returned home to rescue her Teddy bear will also never forget what happened that night in April 1941. Mrs Janet Webb (nee Groves) recalls:

My parents Bert and Freda Groves had lived at Number 19 Padwell Road since their marriage in July 1937. My father was an electrical contractor and a special constable during the war and he was on duty that night. He was badly burned when he got to our house by the fuel from the crashed Heinkel's engines. I can still recall arriving back at the house after our usual overnight stay in Testwood, Totton, and seeing all the mess. Someone – it may have been a chap from the grocery store opposite our house – sifted through the bricks and handed me my Teddy bear. After the incident we all went to live at my grandmother's house in Lodge Road but we still went to stay with the Testwood family at night. I kept the bear until I was a teenager but I still have the two vases my mother found amid the rubble. We also kept the small metal tag with the aircraft number on it for many years but that was cleared when my mother died in 1987. Our house, Number 19, was actually owned by my grandfather, Arthur James Broomfield, who wanted to rebuild it after the war, but it was compulsory purchased to enable the Padwell Day Centre to be built.

Mrs Margaret Kennedy, grand-daughter of the Mortlocks who lived at Number 12 Padwell Road, has equally vivid memories. She recalls:

left: **Little Janet Groves and her father Bert who was injured when the Heinkel crashed in Padwell Road, Southampton.**

Nan and Gramps – Kate and Fred Mortlock – never returned to Padwell Road after the Heinkel destroyed their home. They went to live opposite my parents and me in Ringwood and after the war they came to live with us in Archery Road, Woolston. I have so many memories of that old house in Padwell Road which is now a residential home. In particular, there was an old Morris Oxford or Cowley that Grandad dumped at the bottom of the garden after he stopped driving. He used to let me play on it. He also had this old seat just outside the back door and I used to sit on it with my sister, Kathleen.

I think Nan and Gramps moved into the old house during the 1920s and my sister and I would go over every Saturday and they would look after us. We would all listen to In Town Tonight on the wireless. They were forced out in the end because of the bombing. I remember Granny was ill much of the time and Grandad looked after her. Her sister, Nell, lived opposite and next door to the Royal Arms

left: **The Mortlocks in the back garden of 12 Padwell Road: Kate Mortlock (left) and Fred Mortlock (holding dog). In the middle is their son, Gordon, Margaret Kennedy's father. Seated is Kate Mortlock's mother, Mrs Sarah Heller.**

far right: Freda and Bert Groves at the front door of 19 Padwell Road, Southampton.

right: Janet Groves in the garden at 19 Padwell Road, Southampton.

pub which is still there. Nell used to come over to Nan's during the bombing but it was getting worse and worse. They headed for Exeter to stay with one of their sisters in the end — taking just a small suitcase and a dog called Royal who was named after the pub across the road where he was born. I have lovely childhood memories of life with my wonderful grandparents. But they are tinged with sadness after what happened to the old house.

The incident in Padwell Road during April 1941 was an unusual interlude during a year of sporadic, monotonous bombing which followed the apocalyptic "Blitz Weekend" of November 30, 1940. The New Year had begun with the sight of a thousand incendiaries once again raining down on the town. On this occasion, fire crews dealt with them so quickly that by the time the bombers arrived there was no visible target upon which to dump their high explosives. The same happened ten days later when large numbers of bombers swarmed overhead, raising fears of a repeat of the November 1940 carnage. Yet nothing came of it and the air fleet departed without dropping its bombs.

On the last day of January 1941, Prime Minister Winston Churchill made a secret visit to Southampton with Harry Hopkins, special envoy to President Roosevelt. The President's strong belief that Britain could survive the Blitzkrieg had been influenced by Hopkins'

right: January 1941: Prime Minister Winston Churchill visits Southampton. He mounted the steps of the Civic Centre, turned to the assembled crowd and asked: "Are we downhearted?" The crowd roared back with a defiant "No!"

reports on civilian morale. Churchill was also impressed when he arrived in Southampton.

He would later write to the Minister of Home Security, Herbert Morrison, stating that Southampton's courage should be rewarded with the elevation of the Mayor to the status of Lord Mayor.

The terror, meanwhile, continued. In February, a baby girl and her 82-year-old grandmother were killed. The Southern Daily Echo stated the girl, Isobel, was in the lounge with Grandma when the bomb fell. It then adds with a detached matter-of-factness: "Isobel was blown through the French window into a lily pond, where her body was found by wardens." The baby's mother had been sitting nearby in an armchair which was blown over in the blast and probably saved her life. The report states the child's father discovered the tragedy when he turned his car into the driveway and the headlamps illuminated the carnage.

Next, on March 11, most of the few remaining buildings in Above Bar were damaged or destroyed in a heavy raid. This time fire crews could not contain three fires caused by incendiaries and the area was consequently well marked for aerial bombardment. Sixteen bombers attacked, killing twenty-two people and

left: Margaret Kennedy (nee Mortlock) and dog Royal pictured in the centre with her nanny (left) and sister Kathleen (right). Margaret still has vivid memories of life in Padwell Road before the famous bomber crash in April 1941.

injuring fifty-seven. The next night, the Harland and Wolff ship repair shops were hit and the supply of drinking water was affected when a bomb went through the reinforced concrete roof at the Glen Eyre reservoir.

Twenty-fours later, bombs fell on the suburbs and the British American Tobacco Factory in Millbrook was engulfed by flames. Six people died in the attack. During this raid, a 2,000-pound bomb landed on Alec Bennett's motor garage at Portswood, creating a 10 metre crater where the workshop once stood and sending forty cars into the air. One car hit the side of the Broadway Cinema while other vehicles were flung into nearby gardens. Just beyond the lip of the crater, a family of five had miraculously survived inside their shelter even though one of the cars landed upside-down on

left: The scene in Above Bar, March 1941. The German press had just announced that Southampton was the 4th most bombed target after London, Liverpool and Birmingham.

right: Parachute mine aftermath: The damage caused by the parachute mine raid on April 10, 1941 is evident from this photograph of Derby Road, taken the following morning. One of the twelve mines fell here while other locations included the area between Ludlow and Millais Roads, Howard's Timber Yard, Bitterne Manor, St Mary's Place, Norwich Road, Priory Road and Bitterne Road.

top of it (see photograph below). The family shelter was only 7 metres from the point of impact yet the only casualty was a cat caught under a concrete wall.

When April arrived, twelve parachute mines dropped in pairs during a night raid on the 10th hit a timber yard, a riverside wharf and the suburbs. These bombs, nicknamed "Express Trains" and containing a ton of high explosive, did

colossal damage. Yet the shelters held out and remarkably there was just one fatality. Over forty homes were totally destroyed however.

The town was not so lucky during the following month.

On May 10, 1941 – the day the London Blitz witnessed its tragic finale – Southampton's citizens had gone to bed after hearing the "Raiders Passed" signal

right: Behind the Broadway Cinema where Alec Bennett's garage was destroyed in March 1941.

at 1.23am. When the warning came again ninety minutes later, many chose to stay put and didn't return to their shelters. Others didn't get there in time as more horror hurtled through the sky towards them. Six minutes later twelve bombs fell and ten people were killed. Several were buried alive in the wreckage of their homes in Albert Road, where rescue operations went on for ten hours.

During June 1941 – a crucially significant month during which Hitler turned on Russia – more bombing misery was endured in Southampton. In one appalling tragedy on the 26th, eleven people were killed in the same suburban house as they met to discuss a family wedding. The engaged couple, William Moore and Florence Morant (both 21), died with the bride-to-be's parents, Winifred and Phillip, and her siblings, Sidney, 15, Reginald, 12, twins Elsie and Norman, 9, and Leonard, 8. Two visitors to the house in Northam Bridge Road, Hedge End – Gladys Martin, 23, and her young son Kenneth, 2 – also perished. Mrs Sheila White (nee Morant) was the sole survivor. She recalls:

I was only 6 and was there to be fitted out as a bridesmaid. My aunt, Winifred, was out in the garden and saw the bomb coming down. I believe it was a parachute mine. She then ran indoors and threw herself on top of me which saved my life. The only thing salvaged from the wreckage was my bridesmaid's dress. I was severely injured and my left arm is still covered in scars.

A newly-planted woodland, close to where the house once stood, is to be named Morant Copse after the family.

Another incident that month saw Gwen Hughes – the woman who had been dug out of the Melbourne Restaurant with her children, Gloria and Anthony, – once again have a narrow escape. She recalls:

We were now staying in Rownhams away from the town. One night at 6pm, a lot of planes came over and we were all in the shelter in the garden. I had just gone back indoors to get a cushion to make us more comfortable when a bomb dropped and literally blew me back into the shelter. No-one was hurt, thankfully. My husband Monty (the fireman who had narrowly escaped death when members of his crew were killed in Palmerston Park on November 23, 1940) came to get me. The men at the fire station said they had never seen him move so fast when he heard I was in trouble yet again. Of course, it was not the first time because my husband had rescued the children and me from the Melbourne Restaurant

in the previous November. The other firemen used to laugh about the fact that the bombs seemed to follow me around! When this raid was over, we turned on the radio and Lord Haw-Haw was on. (Haw-Haw, with his quasi upper-crust accent, was in fact American-born William Joyce, who lived in Germany and broadcast from Hamburg as part of the Hitler propaganda team. He could pull in audiences of six million with his "Germany Calling" broadcasts.) He announced that Southampton Docks had just been destroyed. We concluded the Germans must have mistaken Rownhams Lane for the dock area and everyone found that hilarious at the time. But it was another lucky escape for me.

Three images from the barbaric Russian Front: far left: Distraught Russian children: left: Wounded Red Army officer urges his men onwards and right: Freezing German troops. Hitler had postponed Operation Sea Lion, the England invasion, yet again in July 1941 until the spring of 1942 "by which time the Russian campaign will be completed." Then, on February 13, 1942, Admiral Erich Raeder, whose Navy would ferry the invading army across the Channel, discussed Sea Lion with Hitler and got him to at last agree a complete stand-down.

Others were not so lucky that night. The Southern Daily Echo quoted one eyewitness who said: "I went across the road and sitting on a pile of debris near a badly damaged shelter was a grieving woman. She was in a very distressed state, and appeared to be injured. She pointed to the shelter and said: 'My husband and baby are down there.'" The child was two days old. The paper also reported the somewhat bizarre case of a bomb that crushed a man's legs but failed to explode. The man survived.

There was no let-up in July, 1941, either. On the 22nd, 100 warplanes were spotted over Hampshire and incendiaries were dropped north-east towards Romsey. Parachute mines followed causing damage to the Central Railway Station, the Royal Pier, the docks, an army vehicle park at Stoneham Golf Club and also Taunton's School – then an army billet. Twenty lost their lives and 350 people were evacuated from homes.

During the second week of August, fifty bombers attacked from the north and north-west, dropping 5,000 blazing incendiaries and 130 high explosive bombs. The raid was short but devastating. More than 100 fires were started including a massive blaze at Northam where 5,000 gallons of petrol went up in flames; the Central Railway Station was also hit again, ensuring the main line was unusable for several days; the Gas Works was struck and the town went temporarily without gas because the danger of unexploded bombs prevented repair work; three schools and two churches were flattened; and thirty roads, including Commercial Road and New Road, were closed because of craters and unexploded devices. The human cost was also appalling. Thirty-eight people had died.

When the citizens of Southampton turned on their radios in September 1941, a German announcer claimed the town had been left a smoking ruin. In fact, only seven homes in Highfield were still smouldering. Southampton was still intact. Its people were still resolute. Moreover, there would not be another raid on Southampton for six months. The winter lull set in because the prevailing winds of world politics had switched direction. Indeed, as the bitter gusts of winter 1941 blew autumn away, the climate of world war had fundamentally changed.

Hitler was now pursuing a glorious dream, one inspired by the man he idolised. Eighteen months earlier, he had gazed down at the tomb of Napoleon at

the Invalides in Paris. It was, he confided, the "greatest and finest moment in my life". Now his legions were following in Napoleon's footsteps and marching along the old road that Bonaparte had taken to Moscow 129 years earlier. Operation Barbarossa was in full swing. The door of a new 2,000-mile Eastern Front had been ambitiously opened by Hitler. Three German armies – 3.2 million men, thirteen motorised divisions and 3,350 tanks – began carving up the vast Russian hinterland.

At first German progress was good. Hitler wanted Moscow by the end of 1941 – and Leningrad too. However, winter was coming. A bitter, deadly struggle lay ahead and the chaos, drama and savagery of it all would almost defy understanding. Blizzards, mud, and the horror of the Stalingrad siege lay ahead. Fingers would freeze and rifles would jam. Confident of a quick, decisive victory, few Germans had more than summer clothing, and frostbite would soon claim an agonising toll. So many corpses would litter the frozen wastes that it would prove impossible to count them. It was literally a campaign in which no prisoners were taken and the Eastern Front became, for the Germans, a byword for death. To be transferred to the Front was the fate feared most by all German servicemen.

The untold barbarism that was about to unfold would see German corpses used to fill potholes in the road and help armies to cross waterlogged fields.

Starving Russians would resort to cannibalism and to foraging in cemeteries to eat the remains of the recent dead. At the end of this 1,418-day slaughter, the lives of more than 20 million people would be lost.

All that, however, was the future. Now, in the present, air power was needed for the new campaign. The bulk of Goering's Luftwaffe had steadily drifted east since the Russian Front had opened on June 22, 1941, to provide the aerial muscle for Operation Barbarossa.

As 1941 drew to a close, Southampton and the towns and cities of Britain were therefore reprieved while another disturbing fault line appeared in the edifice of the Third Reich. While Hitler concentrated his aerial resources on the Eastern Campaign, Southampton enjoyed a bomb-free winter. Nothing fell for half-a-year. Moreover, the Fuehrer's plans for a British invasion would soon be scrapped.

Two key dates in late 1941 are now important to benchmark. On December 6, Hitler's troops began to be beaten back from the suburbs of Moscow. They had been just fifteen miles from the Kremlin and then the temperature plummeted to minus 40 degrees F. The Germans, paralysed by cold, could not aim their rifles. Hitler ordered them to hold firm and his men fought to a standstill in an inhuman bloodbath that drenched the snow red. On the next day, December 7, an event occurred on the other side of the earth which was to transform the European war – and create another crack in Hitler's Reich. Japanese bombers attacked the US Pacific Fleet at its Pearl Harbour deep-water base on the Hawaiian island of Oahu.

Hitler had been caught as much on the hop in Berlin as apparently Roosevelt had in Washington. The Fuehrer, already bogged down in Russia's bloody quagmire, had made a solemn secret promise to Japan. The fateful pledge, made quite casually and unprompted in 1941, was that Germany would join Japan in a conflict against America. It was time either to honour that promise or to break it. Hitler now compounded his reckless pledge by making the monumental miscalculation of declaring war on America on December 11, 1941. He was too ignorant and Goering too arrogant to understand the potential military strength of the United States. Hitler, who six months earlier had faced only beleaguered Britain, was now allied with Italy and Japan against the three greatest industrial powers in the world – Britain, Russia and America. The Fuehrer hence entered 1942 with a growing logistical and deployment headache.

Southampton, meanwhile, enjoyed the period of calm provided by Hitler's diversion of aerial resources to the Russian Front. The peace was broken when bombers returned in the small hours of April 17, 1942, and caused minor damage to suburban homes. Seven bombers then returned and dumped their payload, claiming five lives. Nine days later, Hitler addressed the German people, telling them British towns and cities would be eradicated "one by one" in revenge for RAF attacks on Germany. The German press referred to the Baedeker Tourist Guide and newspapers discussed marking off each British location within the book as they were destroyed. The raids that followed – openly described as "Terrorangriffe", or "Terror" attacks – became known as "Baedeker Raids" in both Germany and Britain.

Two such raids occurred in Southampton in May 1942 before a third on June 22 signalled the last heavy assault on the town. Some twenty enemy aircraft attacked and fifty bombs were dropped amid flares and thousands of cascading incendiaries. The eastern part of the town was well illuminated and thirty-six people were killed, most as they crouched in shelters. One hundred and sixty homes were destroyed and more than 21,000 damaged.

Yet the Third Reich, the way of life that Hitler declared would last a thousand years, was beginning violently to implode. During 1942, the RAF began a full-scale bombing offensive against German cities (starting with Cologne in May) and the year was to witness two of the war's great turning points.

First, the cruel Eastern Front. The Germans had reached the northern suburbs of Stalingrad on August 23. The most savage battle of the war – an orgy of killing – erupted in the doorways, stairwells and basements as the Russian city was reduced to a ruin. In November, the Russians launched a massive counter-offensive and by the end of the year the Germans were finished. On January 31, 1943, General Paulus' German Sixth Army HQ sent its last message: "The Russians stand at the door of our bunker. We are destroying our equipment." Paulus defied Hitler's orders to fight to the death and surrendered leaving the ranting Fuehrer to insist the General should have shot himself in shame. The battle was the first major loss suffered by the Germans in Europe.

Secondly, by the beginning of November 1942, it was also clear that Hitler had lost the Battle of El Alamein in North Africa, where the British Eighth Army now set about expelling the Germans from Africa altogether. Hitler's world was closing in.

Meanwhile, Southampton's bombing ordeal was almost over as Hitler found himself plugging more and more holes, only to discover new leaks springing up. In fact, the nation's Blitz ordeal would soon peter out completely. Southampton, the town that refused to die, would now survive. Moreover, the ruined town was about to launch an historic and spectacular offensive of its own. The children of the Blitz, the young ones who had endured so much, would be on the streets to watch it happen.

CHAPTER 8

Come back and live with me in America, Rita

Southampton strikes back, 1943–1945

Brian Simpson was ready to take on the Germans. He had the skill. He certainly had the nerve. He could strip down a Sten gun with his eyes shut and re-assemble the intricate parts in seconds. He knew everything there was to know about rifles and his shooting technique was pretty impressive, too. Brian could even lay his hands on a grenade if the need arose.

However Brian wasn't a hardened war veteran. He wasn't even a soldier. He was just a 13-year-old boy. As the tide of war slowly turned against Hitler, some Southampton children seemed adequately prepared to join the fray themselves. Local boys not only managed to collect, trade and swap a bewildering array of weapons and souvenirs. Their knowledge of weaponry and enemy aircraft was often superior to that of adults, too. Brian, the boy who had witnessed the chilling aftermath of the Houndwell Park shelter bombing back in November 1940, recalls:

My dad was a platoon commander in the Home Guard and our house in Oaktree Road, Bitterne Park, was well-equipped to say the least. Dad kept a Sten gun and a rifle at home. There was also a live hand grenade kept beneath a bucket at the end of the garden. It was kept there in case of emergencies and covered simply to ensure it didn't get wet. Dad taught me how to dismantle the Sten gun and I could strip it down while blindfolded and put it back together again. When I was asked what I wanted for

left: **Young Brian Simpson (left) and friend Frank Arthur.**

below: **Brian's father, Thomas, (front) a lieutenant in the Home Guard Hampshire Regiment, 12 Battalion, Southampton East.**

my birthday I remember replying: "A hand grenade, please!" I actually got a handy rubber cosh which commandoes used and I was chuffed to bits with it. I also had a First World War revolver and three rounds which I had bought from another boy for half-a-crown (12.5p). I set up a target on the shelter next door — it was an unoccupied house — and actually fired one round at it. I managed to sneak out and shoot it one night and I don't think anyone noticed because people were always hearing those sorts of noises during the Blitz. I swapped the gun for an American bayonet in the end and that was a real gem, too.

There was nothing particularly unusual about all this. All the boys had similar stuff — they used to haul their goodies around in sacks trying to trade them. Once we got hold of some bullets. I set a dustbin alight and dropped them in one by one and hid round the corner to hear the bang. Then I grabbed the whole lot and threw them in and the whole bin went up with a huge explosion. On another occasion, we found the cartridge and detonator from one of the Bofor anti-aircraft guns. My pal Frank Arthur held the cartridge and I hit the detonator with a hammer and nail. The thing shot up in the sky and frightened us half to death. We loved collecting those sorts of things. The bombing had tailed off by now and they were very exciting days.

The children's excitement was understandable. The air was thick with anticipation. Something big was going to happen. A vast undercover operation seemed to be underway. However the youngsters had no idea exactly what was happening. They had no idea that they, the children of the Blitz, would soon witness history in the making. The destiny of nations was about to unfold before them. Wide-eyed, they would soon experience the build-up to one of the greatest military operations of all time and preparation for the greatest sea-borne invasion in history.

The preliminary and bloody groundwork had been laid during 1943. German resistance in North Africa had completely collapsed in May; the Russian Red Army had clawed its way back from the threshold of annihilation and was now forcing a German retreat; and by January 1944, Allied troops had landed in Nazi-occupied Italy. The time was fast approaching for the Allies to invade German-occupied France and drive towards Berlin as the Russians approached from the opposite direction.

The invasion operation would be called "Overlord", a name chosen by Churchill from a selection of prospective code words. It would happen on June 6, 1944, a date termed "D-Day" - military jargon for any day on which a crucial operation is planned. The objective was simple: the liberation of an enslaved continent from tyranny. It was, by any standards, a hugely ambitious proposal. Invasion would require the breaching of what Hitler called his "Atlantic Wall" - 2,500 miles of fortified coastline from the Bay of Biscay to the northern tip of Norway. The success of Overlord would also crucially depend on the central South Coast ports. Southampton, the town that for so long had been on the defensive, now went spectacularly on the offensive together with Portsmouth, Poole and Portland.

The planning for an eventual return to Europe had its origins as far back as the early summer of 1940. Most people's thoughts at that time were focused on Germany's expected invasion of Britain, but Churchill, the Prime Minister of a few weeks, was even then initiating the first planning stages for an invasion of Europe. By the summer of 1942, Southampton had been surveyed by the War Office and Admiralty as a possible base from which to launch the historic invasion. The conclusion reached was that the town would indeed provide one of the essential springboards from which

left: Life goes on in a Southampton street while American military hardware builds up. There was now a sense that the tide was about to turn. However all households awaited the arrival of bad news about serving loved ones. "I used to dread it," said one telegram boy. "I just pushed the message through the letter box and pedalled away as fast as I could before the screaming and shouting rent the air."

millions of Allied troops would leave the free world and reclaim Nazi-occupied Europe. First the vast troop deployment had to be assembled. Some two million ground forces would be required, of which 176,000 would take part in the initial landings.

The first American GIs (so named because of the initials for Government Issue that appeared on their equipment) had come into Britain via Belfast in March 1942. Now the great Southampton liners Queen Mary and Queen Elizabeth – each capable of carrying more than 15,000 troops – left New York and began bringing thousands of American GIs into Britain for the D-Day operation. They began to pour into Southampton.

In May 1943, the Allies made Operation Overlord their number one priority and during the summer an American unit – "Headquarters 14th Port" – arrived in Southampton to organise the handling of incoming men and cargo. Their HQ was first set up at Maritime Chambers in the Old Docks but later moved to a wing of the Civic Centre.

One of the first Americans in Southampton was horrified by the derelict state of the town. Lieutenant Colonel William Dorn later stated: "I couldn't believe what I saw. Below Bar was absolutely levelled. Virtually nothing was standing, except for one cinema, if my memory serves me right. But the spirit of the people was magnificent. I have never seen such optimism. The British taught the Americans how to accept a war."

The area from Hedge End in the east to Sparsholt in the west became designated "Area C" by the military and within this zone a number of large transit camps were set up to house the invasion army. The docks also began to witness an intense increase in activity as the tools of the war trade steadily built up. Southampton soon became, according to one witness, "one vast camp, dump and airfield". For miles in all directions, every road was crowded with guns, tanks, jeeps, transporters, cranes and the assorted paraphernalia of war.

There was huge competition for limited space. Not only was it the port's duty to accommodate the men and weapons of war. It also had to facilitate secret construction projects. The Allied invasion force would, for example,

be taking its own artificial floating harbours across the Channel in sections to be assembled off the Normandy beaches. Southampton became the main "Mulberry Harbour" construction centre and two were built in seven months – each the size of Dover Harbour and each consisting of two million tons of steel. Part of the ravaged Supermarine works also became the main base of "Force Pluto", an audacious initiative to lay a pipeline on the Channel bed through which fuel would be pumped to the Allied war machine. The Pluto (Pipe Line Under The Ocean) scheme was to succeed in laying twenty pipes after D-Day.

Troops, landing craft and war machines were crammed in wherever there was space. Bulldozers moved into the 1940 Blitz sites, levelling them as quickly as possible for military vehicle parking. As in the Great War, Southampton Common was taken over by the military and camps set up in the northern half and near Cemetery Road. Camouflage netting was strung between the trees to completely cover The Avenue.

When the headquarters staff of the American units arrived, many buildings were requisitioned as the build-up went on. A US unit was housed in the Star Hotel and in a hutted camp at the end of the High Street. There were also US quarters at Ascupart School and at the Territorial Army Centre in Totton.

All the secondary schools were also taken over as mortuaries in preparation for casualties while others – such as King Edward VI Grammar and the Girls' Grammar School – became barracks. Taunton's School was prepared as a prisoner-of-war camp. Arrangements were then made for the injured. The Shadow Hospital, which had been in the vaults beneath Scrase's Brewery, was prepared by the Americans for their wounded and the vast Royal Victoria Hospital at Netley was handed to them, too. It was so large that jeeps were driven along the corridors. The Royal South Hants and Borough General meanwhile restricted admissions in preparation for the inevitable D-Day casualties.

As the day of invasion drew nearer, "Area C" was sealed off with wire fences which prevented access to the sprawling military encampment. In March 1944, movement was also restricted within a ten-mile coastal strip of land from Norfolk to Lands End. This zone was

closed to all visitors and guards were placed at rail stations, bus depots and on roads leading to the area.

Southampton was buzzing. Local children loved the Americans and the town was full of them on the eve of Operation Overlord. Youngsters found them warm, open, gregarious and, most importantly, very generous. The Americans had Lucky Strike cigarettes and wartime rarities such as razor blades, good quality soap, Hershey bars, Coca Cola, tinned fruit and coffee. For women who had endured a wartime ban on silk stockings, there were also US nylons.

The troops gave children endless supplies of chocolate, doughnuts, gum, loose change (and perhaps a softball if they were lucky) to accompany a new repertoire of greetings.

"Gotta sister, mister?" was a useful tack for the Americans to employ with boys who in turn would reply: "Got any gum, chum?" or "Got any candy, Andy?" They would invariably be showered with gum and jaws would ache with over-enthusiastic chewing. Young ladies were treated to various chat-up lines including: "Hiya beautiful, do you like chicken? Then grab a wing!" A familiar, alternative favourite to lure Southampton's teenagers was: "Gee, you look cute, babe. No kiddin'."

A new world of unique experiences also opened up to schoolchildren. Apart from the new banter and gifts, some were also ferried around Southampton in US army hardware. One contributor recalls once seeing a boy emerge from a tank outside the school gates, much to the amazement of his friends. He had been offered a lift to avoid a downpour.

For other youngsters, the arrival of the Americans was educational. Many had never even seen a black person before except in books and film shows. Now they were discovering their culture and music. In dance halls, the music of Glenn Miller

above: American troops marching to Southampton Docks for embarkation to the Normandy landing beaches of Omaha and Utah. The D-Day operation was formidable. It was the equivalent of shifting a city the size of Birmingham over the Channel and moving it towards Paris and then Berlin.

and Benny Goodman ensured the jive, jitterbug and boogie-woogie replaced the waltz and foxtrot.

The new guests also laid on entertainment for the hosts. A huge Christmas party was organised by the US forces at the American Red Cross Club in the High Street in 1943. Three hundred lucky youngsters attended. The Southern Daily Echo reported: " A twelve-foot-high Christmas tree, gaily decorated with coloured lights and lengths of coloured popcorn, stood in the corner of the room in which the party was held. The entertainment consisted of conjuring by Professor W.H. Woodley, ventriloquism by Petty Officer A.G Spicer, singing and dancing by Edna McCrindle and community singing led by Mr Judd. The highlight of the afternoon was the arrival of Father Christmas (impersonated by Corporal Adam Szukalewicz) from a specially-built fireplace. He presented each child with a packet of candy and a packet of cookies and fruit – all given by the Americans from their rations – and a toy."

Al Donovan, the "Swamp Boy" who had watched pilot James Nicolson earn his VC during the Spitfire Summer of 1940, recalls:

We kids loved the Americans. The way they talked and the way they looked was so different. There were some great larger than life characters too. They would always give you all the banter – things like "Hi there, Joe. What do you know?" – and we used to entertain them. I remember my great pal Jack – my playmate from the Swamp Woods – once got hold of his Uncle Stan's big bicycle. He got on it first, and then another lad got on his shoulders and then a third sat on the crossbar. A fourth sat on the handlebars and someone else stood on the front spindle. I would then push them off before getting on the rear spindle myself. All six of us careered down Hill Lane and the Yanks down there loved it. They laughed and cheered, said it was a "swell act" – and of course gave us sweets and gum. They are great, great memories.

Ronald Lyons, the boy who cowered in a pillbox in Chapel Road during the third Supermarine raid in 1940, recalls:

It was unbelievable in the town in the month before D-Day. I used to go down there with my friends and look at them. There was a huge mass of US tanks at the approach to the Pier and the line stretched all the way back to the Civic Centre. They also had two camps – one for the black Americans and one for the white ones. All of them would give us sweets and throw us loose change. I think they were using us as a way to get to our mums. I'll tell you something, though. It wasn't all great. The town began to stink down there after a while. There were so many of them camped there and the place reeked of urine. There were also fights caused by jealousy because the Yanks looked so elegant and smart in their posh gabardine uniforms whereas our soldiers had rough, badly-made clothes. They also had money and this all led to a lot of resentment. The girls were throwing themselves at the Americans and there were punch-ups between our lads and theirs. I used to see them down by the Bargate and once I saw an American punched right through a pub window.

Recorded in the official "14th Port Books" are thirty-one cases of fighting between American and British military personnel (with some brawls involving knives) and twenty-seven between white and black Americans. To curb trouble, British soldiers were prevented from carrying knives outside barracks and American and British military police patrols stepped up. Even so, one American was court-martialled for murder and one for manslaughter.

The incidence of road accidents increased dramatically during this period – and so did venereal disease cases. Clinics were set up as the number of women patients suffering from sexually transmitted diseases rose markedly. There was a steady increase in cases of girls under 15 and in the 15-20 age group. Many were "camp followers", prostitutes from outside the area who rented rooms in the town and found customers on trams and buses.

The American troops were kept under control by their own military police, a tough gun-carrying squad nicknamed the "Snowdrops" after their spotless white helmets. They were based in Nissen huts on Hoglands Park in a camp known as "Hut City" by the locals. The "Snowdrops" had a direct, no nonsense approach to trouble and had no reservations about striking out with truncheons when violence flared.

Meanwhile, Brenda Logie, the 20-year-old entertainer, now found herself singing to the town's new guests. She recalls:

"On the eve of D-Day everything was so secret. We were taken in covered lorries to entertain so that even we couldn't work out where some of the New Forest camps were. Another thing that struck you was the segregation of the black and white Americans. The whites were down in the port and the blacks were in the old Victorian Ordnance Office (now the new law courts) which had lots of passageways inside the building. One of the white officers later told me that three "ladies of the night" from Portsmouth had been inside the Ordnance Office for four months and no-one had found them! When there had been inspections, the girls simply disappeared to somewhere else in the building and they were never seen. I don't know what happened to the girls in the end but there was a hell of a fuss about it when it was discovered what had been going on.

The white Americans didn't like us white girls even talking to the blacks because it wasn't allowed in some parts of America. The whites and blacks fought a lot and, of course, our boys fought with them too. I sang for everyone. The Americans were a lot noisier and always came up very close to the stage to stare at you when they danced. They would just sway together and look at you. It was quite strange really. The old saying about them — over-sexed, over-paid and over here — was basically true. They loved going to the dances — the Guildhall was very popular— and young girls liked dancing with them. I also remember that Bassett Green Road was filled nose to tail with tanks from a Canadian Regiment. When you were going to work in the morning, you would see them sitting beside their tanks and brewing a cuppa. They would hang their shaving mirrors on the guns too. There were a lot of American Indians among them. I also recall the American officers going round local houses asking if the Indians could come in for a bath. The Indians didn't talk to anyone so the officers spoke on their behalf.

My last memory was a few days before they all left for D-Day. Just before the invasion occurred in June 1944, the Americans took over the Ballroom of the Polygon Hotel and gave their enlisted men a day of entertainment. They had films in the morning and a concert in the afternoon, at which I sang, and then a dance in the evening.

Jean Thorn, the little evacuee who went on the run from Christchurch, was now 16. She recalls:

I had come out of one of the picture houses with a friend and an American woman approached us and asked if we would like to entertain the white GIs. We became hostesses at the Americans' Red Cross Club in the High Street. Our job was to make them feel at home but we were not allowed to date them or even give them our addresses. It was very strict like that. We simply chatted to them and danced with them and had a great time. They taught me to jitterbug! Some of the Americans were hillbillies who couldn't read or write. So we spent a lot of time reading their mail for them and helping them to write back. Their club was very posh with lovely carpets and highly polished wood — not a bit like the places where our troops had to go. The Americans also had a barracks in Millbrook Road where we lived and, because we were one of the only occupied houses in the street, they came round all the time. They used to gather round the fire in the lounge telling stories or playing cards. We used to have parties too and they would bring mountains of food over. We must have been the best-fed family in Southampton! They were so generous and really lovely people. They were also true gentlemen as far as women were concerned. I ended up with lots of marriage proposals!

The war was now about to enter its critical phase and the Allied invasion of France on June 6, 1944, would be both the emotional and strategic climax of the conflict. By the end of April, the assault troops had moved to their sealed embarkation areas – known as "sausages" because of their shapes on the map. These areas geographically corresponded with the areas of Normandy where they were scheduled to land. The Americans, for example, occupied the West Country to line them up with the westernmost sections of the invasion coast – the beaches code-named Utah and Omaha.

British and Canadian troops would sail from Southampton and land at Gold, Juno and Sword beaches.

It was planned to move the invaders from British ports and across the Channel with 5,300 ships and other craft, the largest fleet ever assembled. The greatest aerial armada in history, some 12,000 planes, would also land major elements of three airborne divisions in Normandy to keep the Germans at bay while the landing craft approached. Six infantry

right: The Americans approach Normandy. They had begun the invasion at Utah and Omaha beaches one hour before the British landed. Utah had been strangely quiet because the invaders were in the wrong position. A powerful current had dragged the force a mile south of the intended landing site where, by chance, the beach was almost unprotected. However 10 miles away, at Omaha, German veterans of the Eastern Front were waiting. Within 10 minutes every officer and sergeant in the first wave was killed or wounded. Others simply sat crying in total shock. Omaha was a near disaster yet a toehold was gained. It was easier overall on the British eastern beaches but not everywhere and localised tragedies and horrors unfolded here too.

divisions – three American, two British and one Canadian – would then attack a sixty-mile stretch between Caen and Cherbourg.

On May 23, 1944, all military camps on Southampton Common were completely sealed off and armed guards kept prying eyes at bay. Eight days later, landing craft were loaded up in a four-day operation which was completed in time for Churchill to inspect the invasion armada. On June 5, 1944, the Southampton fleet began to move out and assemble off the Isle of Wight, where similar fleets from Plymouth, Portland and Portsmouth were also heading.

On the eve of the great day, Southampton "knew in its bones that a climax was at hand, despite the veil of secrecy that shrouded the coming operations", wrote Bernard Knowles in his war history. He added: "…Without trumpets, the vast concourse of assault ships drew slowly away from Southampton Docks and, like a moving mosaic – 'the ships were so close together', writes an eyewitness, 'that it looked for all the world as though one could walk all the way to the Isle of Wight without wetting one's feet'

– sailed without let or hindrance down Southampton Water to take up its place at the appointed rendezvous as the core of the invasion fleet."

Knowles continued: "Thereafter, with every street full of excited whispers, the people of Southampton, intuitively aware of the greatness of the hour, but still in ignorance as to the true facts, suffered an agony of suspense. That same night it was heightened when, silhouetted against a sky of dull pearl, watchers saw what, in the words of one observer, looked like 'strings of sharks'. In reality they were Dakota-towed gliders heading for the Channel on the first stage of the most desperate military venture of all time."

At 6.31am on June 6, 600 American GIs from the 4th Division leapt from landing craft ramps into waist-deep water and began to wade towards Normandy's Utah beach. An hour later, assault troops from the Second British Army went ashore at Gold, Juno and Sword beaches. At Omaha Beach, hell visited earth when the invaders met a crack German Division. Three thousand Americans lost their lives on the blood-drenched sands.

History and destiny hung in a precarious balance but the Allies were in

Normandy to stay and 156,000 Allied troops waded ashore on D-Day alone. Within days, 600,000 troops were in France. The Third Reich had finally confronted reality – and catastrophe.

Southampton now became a vast thoroughfare through which the essential instruments of liberation passed. During the seventeen weeks that followed D-Day, the military tonnage handled by the docks matched the total imports and exports dealt with in the last complete peacetime year, 1938. Thousands of vessels entered and left the port, millions of tons of freight passed over the quays and three-and-a-half million British, Commonwealth and American troops left the town during the twelve months that elapsed between D-Day and eventual victory in Europe.

Children lined the streets as the endless convoy of troops and machines continued. As the tanks rolled by, American soldiers threw down their rations, their cigarettes and their money. When the columns of armour came to a standstill, the youngsters even clambered aboard the jeeps and lorries for a closer look, peering beneath canvas covers at the ammunition and weapons of war. Logjams of military traffic were also a good opportunity to sell the troops fish, chips and drinks.

Southampton was learning to smile again. The Yanks were here. Townsfolk were more relaxed. The terror from the skies had gone. Or so they thought. A small number of bombs had suddenly fallen in 1943 and then, almost a year later, four people lost their lives – including two wardens – when a ton of explosives fell on Portswood damaging 900 homes. The four who died were to be Southampton's last air raid fatalities.

However, on a July morning in 1944, a secret weapon hurtled towards Southampton at 360mph trailing a plume of yellow exhaust flames. The eight-metre steel cylinder, carrying a ton of high explosives, heralded a new, terrifying age of warfare. An era when buttons could simply be pressed to deliver slaughter. An era which gave birth to cruise and ballistic missiles. It had speed, it had stealth, and it had a range of 150 miles. Most disturbing of all, the new weapon did not require a pilot to carry it.

It was Hitler's new toy: a flying bomb. Some 8,600 would eventually be launched at Britain from catapult ramps in northern France with sufficient gasoline fuel to reach southern England. A spinner system in the nose calculated the distance flown and then a gadget in

SOUTHERN DAILY ECHO, TUESDAY, JUNE 6, 1944.

FINAL

SOUTHERN
Daily Echo

REGISTERED AT THE GENERAL POST OFFICE AS A NEWSPAPER.

TELEPHONE: SOUTHAMPTON 76-81

Three Half-Pence [NEWSPAPER DELIVERY CHARGE EXTRA]

Vol. LVI.—No. 17235   SOUTHAMPTON, TUESDAY, JUNE 6, 1944.

Allies Land in Northern France

EARLY MORNING SURPRISE FOR GERMANS

"Free Men Marching Together to Victory"—*Eisenhower*

KING TO BROADCAST TO-NIGHT

"COMMUNIQUE NUMBER ONE" set the world agog to-day. It was issued from Supreme Headquarters, Allied Expeditionary Force (S.H.A.E.F. for short) at 9.33 a.m., and said:

"Under the command of General Eisenhower, Allied naval forces, supported by strong air forces, began landing Allied armies this morning on the Northern Coast of France."

IN this brief manner the United Nations, their enemies, and quoted on this page.

"LIKE HELL LET LOOSE"
Bridgehead Soon Ours

"TERRIFIC ALLIED TEAM"
Montgomery Confident

EISENHOWER'S Order of the Day

BEFORE the assaulting troops embarked, each man was handed this stirring order of the day, issued by General Eisenhower:

"Soldiers, sailors and airmen of the Allied Expeditionary Force. You are about to embark upon the great crusade towards which we have striven these many months. The eyes of the world are upon you..."

IT'S SCARCE BUT IT'S GOOD!

'Camp' Coffee is scarce because the good coffee, chicory and sugar of which it is made are in short supply. But 'Camp' is still as good and as strong as these good ingredients can make it.

'CAMP' COFFEE
Still of pre-war strength

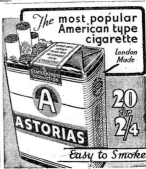

The most popular American type cigarette
London Made

ASTORIAS
20 for 2/4
Easy to Smoke

---

the navigation equipment was tripped, cutting the fuel supply and sending it earthbound. The bomb then plummeted in eerie silence, awaiting its appointment with something solid.

It didn't matter where the bomb landed. That was the point. It was a terror weapon. Hitler's propaganda minister Goebbels had named the Orwellian creation the V1 – the V standing for Vergeltungswaffe or "Vengeance" weapon. Britain knew it variously as the Doodlebug, Buzz Bomb, Robot Bomb or, simply, the Flying Bomb.

left: **Airborne troops on their way to France for Operation Overlord.**

This particular V1 was close to Southampton now and its primitive automatic guidance system would soon send it diving towards humanity. Some 3,000 feet below, ten-year-old Brian Martin and his six-year-old brother Ray were inside the Anderson shelter their father had built in their garden in Swanmore Avenue. Dad was now fighting in Belgium but their mother, Gladys, was inside the cramped corrugated tube with them. Then came the strange sound of a misfiring engine. Then silence. The V1 bomb landed 6 feet (1.8m) from where the Martin family huddled. It was a massive blast which destroyed their two-bedroom semi – and around twenty others in the road. Mr Ray Martin recalls:

Luckily the three of us were down in the shelter as a matter of routine. We went down there every night. There was a whole row of ten Andersons along the gardens and thankfully they probably saved the road's residents. I was only six but can still recall being woken up by a huge noise at around 1am. My mum then cried: "We can't get out." We were probably saved by a blast wall made up from old rabbit hutches filled with earth put up by my grandfather the day before. But those hutches had been blown across the entrance to the shelter.

Neighbours came over to help dig us out and I remember all the fires in the road when we emerged. The bomb actually landed in an orchard which backed on to the garden but the crater it made came right up to where our shelter was positioned. The Anderson must have saved our lives that day. It was a terrible shock to see our house and the road after. A photograph (see opposite) was taken at the time which shows a neighbour standing by our shelter with the destroyed houses behind him. You can also see a bath hanging out of the side of

left: **Men of the Hampshire Regiment in France after D-Day. The 1st Battalion of the Hampshires had been first ashore at Gold Beach and lost 200 men that day.**

above: **A resident poses for the camera amid the wreckage of homes in Swanmore Avenue after the V1 bomb landed. During the raid, the Martin family had been inside their Anderson shelter (to the man's right) showing just how close the family came to being killed.**

above right: **Gladys Martin with her sons, Brian (standing) and Raymond.**

one house which is such an eerie image. Nothing survived in our home. The only thing left from our place was a jar of bottled fruit which had been kept under the stairs. We went to stay with my mum's brother in Bitterne after that but our house was eventually rebuilt and we moved back in. I still think it was amazing we were still all sleeping in the shelters because the bombing had tailed right off and nothing had really happened for a long time.

When the V1 fell in Swanmore Avenue on July 12, 1944 (and another landed in woodland in Bursledon three days later injuring soldiers), there were fears they could signal the start of a new remote-controlled phase of the town's bombardment. The fears were unfounded. London was the principle recipient of the V1 flying bomb and its successor, the high altitude, 4,000mph V2 rocket. Some 8,994 lives would be claimed by the doomsday weapons – mostly civilians living in the capital. However, the two that landed in Southampton marked the end of the town's Blitz and the last recorded "all clear" would sound on November 5, 1944.

Flying bombs were not the only

arrivals in Southampton after D-Day. Huge convoys of trains emblazoned with red crosses brought the first of 222,000 wounded troops into Southampton. The first prisoners-of-war also started arriving at the port's 101 Berth.

A PoW transit centre had been set up in the docks where troops received first aid before being moved to permanent camps inland. Brian Simpson, the young armaments expert, recalls:

I was now 14 and had started work for Vickers. Our bus home went past the German PoW camp that was set up at Chandler's Ford. It had previously been an American base and kept as a D-Day hospital. But overnight the Yanks went and gun turrets and barbed wire sprang up. When the bus went past while the Americans were there, it was all waves and cheers. Now the Germans were there it became v-signs and shouting. I remember the Germans once made life-sized cardboard cut-outs of farm animals and stuck them up in the camp for passers-by to see. It was really very clever and looked excellent but it was still an odd experience on the bus that day.

While wounded Allied troops and German prisoners came in – some 185,000 PoWs entered the port after D-Day – the Americans continued to go out. On October 25, 1944, the "Millionth Yank", 26-year-old Sergeant Paul S. Shimer, of Chambersburg, Pennsylvania, left for Normandy. Within three months another million Americans had followed him. Shimer, a married

man with a three-year-old daughter, was killed in action as the last acts in the tragedy of Nazi Germany unfolded.

On August 25, 1944, the Allies had liberated Paris after four years of German occupation and found French resistance units already largely in control. Six months later, the Russians had reached the German border and the Allies had undertaken a devastating bombing campaign against Germany, flattening Dresden in the process. Soon the British would be at the gates of Hamburg and the Russians and Americans swarming in the suburbs of Berlin. German hopes in promised Nazi "miracle" weapons, which had sustained the masses of the people, had also been abandoned and the launching sites for the V1 flying bombs and the V2 rockets had been captured. Moreover, the project to build a futuristic

breed of Nazi jet fighters went up in smoke as Allied pilots destroyed the extended runways and fuel refineries they needed.

For Hitler, directing his crumbling armies from an underground bunker 50 feet beneath the Berlin Chancellery, it was all over. On April 29, 1945, with the Russian Red Army just streets away from the bunker, the exhausted warlord married his mistress Eva Braun and then dictated his last will and testament. The man who ruled Germany for more than 12 years and most of Europe for four, placed "sole responsibility" for the deaths of millions on the battlefields and in the bombed towns and cities on the Jews. Absolute power had corrupted, deranged and finally destroyed him. His hair was lank and his eyes dull; spittle dribbled from the corners of his mouth

above: **A column of German prisoners at the Royal Pier, Southampton, shortly after D-Day.**

above right: **The PoW transit centre in the New Docks, Southampton, known as "The Cage". August 1944.**

far right: **Architect of the Blitz, Hermann Goering, slumps forward in thoughtful mood during the Nuremberg war trials.**

and his left hand and leg developed tremors. Perched in the corner of a sofa, he continued to dictate memos to non-existent armies and issue execution orders to men who were already dead. The next day, April 30, 1945, ten days after his 56th birthday, Hitler shot himself in the mouth. His wife took poison. Hitler's Reich survived him by just one week, while two atomic bombs in August ended Japanese resistance and the world conflict.

What of the architect of the Blitz, Hermann Goering? He had surrendered himself to the Americans and saw himself as the star defendant when twenty-one Nazi leaders – charged with "crimes against humanity" and "violations of the rules of war" – appeared before an International Military Tribunal in Nuremberg, Germany, in November 1945. Goering – morphine addict, sycophant, collector of flamboyant uniforms and offices of state – was sentenced to death and had his claim for the bullet rather than the noose turned down. He would never see his vast Baronial estate north of Berlin again; he would never marvel at the enormous art collection he kept there; and the 52-year-old father would not see his eight-year-old daughter Edda again either. Two hours before his execution, Hitler's favoured son, his specially appointed "Reich Marshall", swallowed a vial of cyanide poison that had been smuggled into his cell. He died in seconds, deluding himself that he would be laid to rest in a marble sarcophagus and celebrated as a German martyr within fifty years.

In Southampton, the town ravaged by Goering's Luftwaffe, news of Germany's

unconditional surrender at Rheims in France on May 7, 1945, had soon filtered through. Singer Brenda Logie recalls:

I was doing an army show in the Avenue Hall in Southampton and suddenly an officer came on to the stage. Everyone started jeering and telling him to get off but he calmed them down by saying he had something to tell them. He then said the war was over. Some laughed. Some cried. Most didn't know what to do. Then the whole place just erupted. The show I was doing was abandoned and instead we all just sang and sang. The whole hall broke out into "There'll Always Be An England" and "Land of Hope and Glory" and we would have been there all night if they had let us. It was highly emotional and a

left: The millionth American soldier passes through Southampton for Europe on October 25, 1944. He was 26-year-old Sergeant Paul S. Shimer who was to be killed in action six months later. He is pictured being welcomed by the Mayor of Southampton, Cllr R. J. Stranger. In 1947, the former Mayor and his wife visited America and met Paul Shimer's family. R. J. Stranger had started a trust fund in England to help with the education of Shimer's young daughter, Patricia. Shimer came from Chambersburg, an apple growing district in Pennsylvania, and the town gave many gifts of apples and other foods to Southampton schools.

fantastic atmosphere that I'll never forget. Then there was an official weekend of celebrations and the most amazing thing I can recall from the whole period was when all the lights came back on again. We had all lived in darkness up to then due to the blackout and now, all of a sudden, there was this incredible light. It was just like fairyland and it was the real sign that war was over.

Tuesday May 8, 1945, had been set aside for the formal declaration of peace but the celebrations were not waiting until then. The blackout was over and Southampton's evacuated children were on their way home. Now was the time to party. On Monday May 7, American jeeps and lorries toured the town blaring their horns in competition with the sirens of ships docked in the port. Bonfires were prepared on the site of Blitzed properties and at midnight, as the great day came, the town's celebrations erupted. Ship's

above: **Hitler is dead, the Russians are in Berlin and the Reich has collapsed. Allied officers amid the ruins of Berlin.**

centre left:
Celebrating the end of the war: The Bevois Street party in St Mary's, Southampton.

right: **Victory in Europe Day celebration party in New Road, West End, Southampton. The Martin brothers, who survived the V1 bomb when it landed in Swanmore Road, are pictured far left. Raymond is sitting on the end with dark jacket while brother Brian is peering over his left shoulder.**

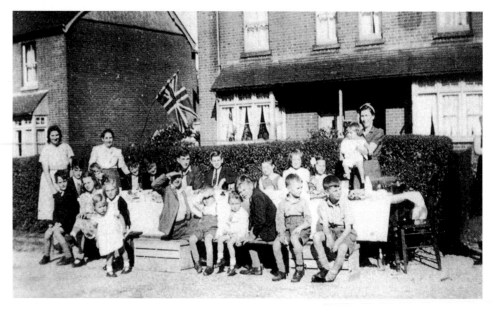

right and below
right: **Two shots of
Victory in Europe
Day at Southampton
Civic Centre. A sailor
carrying a Union Flag
on a pole began a
mass conga which
snaked for half a
mile. Others swam
in the fountain and
performed acrobatics
on top of the flag
poles.**

bottom right:
**Youngsters celebrate
the end of the
war in Northam,
Southampton.**

sirens sounded, searchlights raked the sky, laughter and singing filled the streets and red and green signal rockets illuminated the heavens. That afternoon, 20,000 gathered in front of the Civic Centre to hear a service of thanksgiving and to hear a relay of the Prime Minister's speech to the nation. Then silence as the Guildhall organ played the town's own hymn, "O God Our Help in Ages Past", through loudspeakers. Street parties across the town followed.

The Editor of the Southern Daily Echo told his readers that Nazism was dead and it was time to remember. "So at last," he wrote, "we have come to the end of the road. It has been a long and weary way. Many gallant spirits are not with us to share in the joy of the goal achieved and the victory won. Our first thoughts today are with those who have given their lives so that we may live, and with those who have been bereaved by the ravages of war."

Some Blitz teenagers had other thoughts, however: crossing the Atlantic for a new life.

On January 26, 1946, SS Argentina eased out of the rain-swept New Docks in Southampton and headed for New York. On board were 464 American war brides, sixty-seven babies and 109 other

children. A stormy seven-day voyage lay ahead and, for many, an uncertain future. As the tugs manoeuvred the liner away from her berth, the young brides – many just teenagers – shouted in chorus: "We'll never forget England." Then some sang: "God Bless America." Relatives waved until the ship was a distant speck. More than 70,000 British war brides were to follow them to America and a further 40,000 to Canada.

On February 3, 1946, Queen Mary left Southampton with a further 2,334 wives and children of American servicemen. As the giant 81,000-ton liner left Ocean Dock, young mums waved from the deck-rails and the faces of babies and young children peered through the ship's portholes.

When US Washington left Southampton on April 28, teenage bride Rita Parker was on board. She had lost her mother, two brothers and three sisters when the family shelter was hit in Melbourne Street during the third Supermarine raid on September 26, 1940 (see pages 59-60). Young Rita had only escaped herself after being sent on an errand moments before. Now a new life beckoned. She recalls:

It was a very big step to take, particularly in light of what had happened to the family. I was the only girl left and Dad didn't want me to go. But I had met an American sailor called Harold Kump at one of the Guildhall dances and you could say it was love at first sight. I was only 16 and he was my first real boyfriend. A year later we were married in a house next to the bombed-out St Mary's Church by Canon Jolly and then we left for America. I was really looking forward to trying a different way of life. The journey was fine until about three days out and then there was the most terrible storm. But we got through it and arrived in New York after five-and-a half days. We then went to Grand Central Station and took the train down to Harrisburg in Pennsylvania where Harold came from.

We lived with his parents initially and then he went back to sea in the Merchant Navy. It was all very strange at first. On one of my first days there, Harold's family took me to their Pentecostal church. When I saw all the dancing and how excited everyone got, I nearly passed out. I was amazed. The food was odd at first, too. I remember when I was presented with corn on the cob. I had never seen it before and asked how it should be eaten! Then there were the accents which were so hard to understand – and the money. After about a year, I gradually

above: **Robert Rateau**

right: **Robert Rateau, Joyce Williams and their baby, Lorraine.**

below: **Baby Lorraine.**

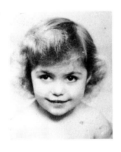

below: **VE day celebration party in Outer Circle, Coxford, Southampton.**

got used to it and adjusted. Unfortunately it didn't work out. Harold had been seeing a girl in California before I came out and he started up with her again. I then discovered she was expecting his child. We divorced after only two years and I weighed up whether I should go home to Southampton. I decided to stay in America and I trained to become an accountant.

Marriage and a new life in America was also offered to teenager Joyce Williams. She had met American serviceman Robert Rateau and was now pregnant. Joyce, who worked at the British American Tobacco factory in Southampton, had already married at 17 but that had not lasted. Now the love of her life was the smart American she had met at a dance at the US Barracks in Millbrook Road. He was a sergeant in charge of catering at the Barracks, which now housed German prisoners. Their baby, Lorraine, duly arrived but several weeks later, Robert Rateau was called back to America with his troop. The new dad begged Joyce to follow him with their child but she did not want to leave Southampton. He even returned to Southampton for several months and tried again to tempt Joyce to start a new life across the Atlantic. She still turned him down and sent her sister to Southampton Docks to inform him that the mother of his child was staying put.

Their daughter Lorraine recalls:

He really wanted mum and I to go over there to Atlanta, Georgia. But we didn't and he died in 1952 at the age of 32 from what I believe was a broken heart. My mother married another man and I grew up thinking this person was my father. I thought

the handsome GI in a photo on the sideboard was simply "Uncle Bob". I was 13 when my mother told me: "Listen, Lorraine, your real dad was an American soldier." She told me he loved me dearly and what had happened. The truth came out because my real father's mother, Alice, had sent a letter to the Salvation Army in a bid to trace her grand-daughter. The letter ended up in my mum's hands and she chose to hand it to me. It was a shattering experience at the time. The whole world had changed. I felt deceived and angry and confused all at once. I remember saying: "I don't want another dad!" I have been told he was a generous, wonderful man with a great sense of humour. He worshipped my mum, Nan and me. I have been over to Atlanta to see my dad's grave and it was a very moving experience. His name is engraved on a pink marble wall and I can't put into words how it felt when I looked at it. I tied some silk roses on to a hook there to let him know his little girl had come back.

Back in post-war Southampton, the war brides had left behind a town in ruins. A terrible price had been paid for Hitler and Goering's lunacy. The hastily typewritten day-to-day reports compiled by the local ARP (Air Raid Precautions) Department were later summarised to give the final number of Southampton fatalities as 631. This official report adds that a further 903 were seriously hurt and 985 injured between 1940-44. The

THE BLITZ:
where the bombs fell

● H. E. Bombs (2,631).   ▲ Parachute Mines (36).   From June, 1940 to September, 1941.

138

right: Bulldozers move in at Supermarine in 1979 to demolish the Main Woolston Works.

truth of the matter is that it's impossible to be precise. The Southern Daily Echo, for example, claimed as early as October 1944 that 633 were killed, 922 seriously hurt and 986 injured. It is safe to assume the real death toll would be much higher still if it was possible to accurately include those who died from their injuries in the months – indeed years – that followed.

Similar problems with accuracy apply to other categories. For example, the same official records show that Goering's Luftwaffe dropped 475 tons of high explosive contained within 2,631 bombs on Southampton plus almost 31,000 incendiaries. However, the Southern Daily Echo figure, published in October 1944, claims bombs weighing 530 tons fell. The masterly research carried out by the "Blitz Then and Now" team (see Bibliography) hikes these figures still further. Certainly, the tonnage which fell on the "warm up" night of November 23, 1940 and the "Blitz Weekend" which followed, was considerably higher than the official statistics suggest – dramatically so in most categories. The team states, for example, that some

left: Legacy of the Blitz: an illustration showing where the bombs fell.

300 tons of high explosive fell during the "Blitz Weekend" alone – three times the official figure for those two nights.

Finally, the official figures state that the town endured fifty-seven attacks over four years leaving 936 homes destroyed and 2,653 so badly damaged they had to be demolished. A further 41,000 homes were in need of some sort of repair. Again these figures appear in need of upward revision.

Bernard Knowles attempted to put a financial value on the residential and industrial damage. He concluded that the town's rateable value dropped by 12.5 per cent during the Blitz – the third biggest percentage fall anywhere outside London. These figures, though difficult to use definitively, give a broad impression of the scale of the Blitz disaster. It was a considerable cost. It was a human tragedy. Yet the town slowly, painfully and determinedly re-emerged from the ashes.

The Southern Daily Echo Editor had set the tone as early as 1940 when he wrote this stirring commentary after the ferocious "Blitz Weekend" raids:

"Southampton has endured a great ordeal. Even as we survey with sorrowful hearts the evil work, we know that Southampton, with a past of over 1,000 years, can look forward to a great future… we shall build anew, not only our houses and shops and our public

buildings, but our social order … In such a world Southampton will once again become the 'Gateway to Britain', the great port from which ships and planes, merchandise and travellers, will reach out to all corners of the world."

The town did build anew. It became a city in 1964 and the city went on to re-establish itself as the "Gateway to Britain". Southampton entered the new millennium as the UK's premier cruise and vehicle handling port and one of the fastest growing terminals in Europe. Its recent renaissance has also included continued redevelopment of its once ruined retail and commercial centre. The vast West Quay shopping mall in Above Bar, opened in 2000, is one of the largest city shopping centres in Britain. The town reduced to ashes in 1940 is today recognized throughout the world as both a great British city and a great international hub port. The foundations were laid by those youngsters who were dug out of rubble, who had lost their parents, whom war had stripped of innocence. It was the children of the Blitz who grew up and found the strength to build a city of the future.

CHAPTER 9

Maurice, Jon and friends remember

Views and conclusions

THE SUN prised its way through the leaden clouds at the precise moment the young boy was mentioned. Warmth momentarily enveloped the crowd as the name of 14-year-old Kenneth Doswell was uttered by the Reverend David Flint. More names followed, including that of 14-year-old Douglas Cruikshank. Then tightly shut eyes for the Lord's Prayer.

High above, the arching span of the toll bridge ferried traffic from one side of the Itchen to the other, its churning waters winking below. Sixty years ago, the Vickers Supermarine factory stood on the spot where the towering structure now delivers vehicles safely to the Woolston side. Sixty years ago to the hour, heavy bombers had flown down this river, dropping bombs and extinguishing life.

They were singing now, the strains of "Oh God Our Help In Ages Past" ebbing and flowing in the strong breeze. Then a respectful silence to remember the dead at the request of Reverend Flint.

Maurice Young was in the crowd. It was his 71st birthday and he had watched the Supermarine catastrophe on the occasion of his 11th. His friend, local historian Jon Honeysett, who had organised the commemorative service, was nearby. When he was five, his grandad had taken him to inspect the shell of the Works and told him: "Your Auntie Ella came out of there alive."

Many survivors were among the

above: **The Supermarine Memorial in Spitfire Walk, Southampton.**

100-plus crowd. Many were lost in thought, others were clearly overcome. The Mayor of Southampton, Cllr Peter Wakeford, now laid a wreath on behalf of 145 Squadron, one of the few Battle of Britain Associations left, upon the small blue memorial plaque which sits by the waterfront. Group Captain David Green laid a second on behalf of the Spitfire Society, the floral arrangement shaped like the famous fighter once made just a stone's throw from where he stood.

A woman then came forward with a single rose. "That's for Peggy," said Mrs Joan Rolfe as she remembered her friend, 19-year-old Supermarine employee Margaret Moon. Peggy had died on September 24, 1940, when a bomb hit the railway arch she was cowering beneath. Two days later Joan, then a 20-year-old typist, prayed for her own life. As the bombs fell again, she had laid on the basement floor under Supermarine's Administration Block with hands over her head and repeated the words of a hymn: "Faint not nor fear, His arms are near." Outside the bombs whistled and the ground heaved beneath her with every crash. Then Joan ran up Sea Road to the Red Lion shelter where women and children were faintly singing "The Woodpecker's Serenade": "Hear him pecking out his melody, peck, peck pecking in the same old key............"

Fast forward to 2000 and the riverside memorial service was over and talk had begun. Old times were relived, hands warmly shaken, memories corrected and loved ones mourned. There was much talk about bravery and endeavour. There was even more concerning remembrance and the lessons of history. Yet what lessons can be learnt from the time when battle raged in the skies and civilians paid the price of war? What conclusions, if any, can be confidently plucked from a murky sea of conflicting evidence, nostalgia, ravaged emotions and acute trauma?

The following observations are offered as a means to making sense of this snapshot in time and to conclude this volume. They are, however, merely personal views presented in chronological fashion in line with the approach adopted during previous chapters. First considered is the aerial Battle of Britain phase from July –September 1940, which Hitler viewed as a necessary German victory before land invasion could be attempted. There then follows scrutiny of the Blitzkrieg on Southampton which unfolded once the aerial phase was lost and German invasion plans thwarted.

Perhaps the most fundamental initial question is: Did Hitler really plan to invade Britain? Hitler had ordered some preliminary planning for a landing and on July 16, 1940, he certainly issued Directive 16 declaring that Operation Sea Lion would go ahead "if necessary". It would be, his generals began to realise, a massive military operation. Many historians have since questioned the seriousness of the operation. It was, some claim, a sham, an elaborate campaign of deception aimed at shielding the genuine policy objective: the invasion of Russia.

Operation Sea Lion was therefore a smokescreen for Operation Barbarossa.

The mysterious character of Rudolf Hess, Hitler's Deputy, has also been usefully employed to support this argument.

It is commonly supposed that his 1,200 mile solo flight from Germany to Glasgow in 1941 was the act of a deluded madman with a crazy notion of single-handedly brokering a peace deal with Britain. Hitler himself officially dismissed Hess in these terms but revisionist historians have consistently sought to push Hess from the sidelines and into the limelight. His role, they say, was pivotal, not peripheral. Hess's melodramatic arrival in Scotland had, they maintain, Hitler's full blessing. Hitler wanted peace with Britain and Hess was negotiating a formal deal. This school argues it was no coincidence that the bombing of Britain tailed off following Hess's arrival indicating the emergence of a virtual truce while the peace talks

top: **The Mayor of Southampton, Cllr Peter Wakeford, and Group Captain David Green, lay their wreaths at the Supermarine Memorial in Spitfire Walk, Southampton, on September 26, 2000.**

above: **Historian Jon Honeysett, who arranged the memorial service, giving a moving speech to the assembled crowd before the wreath-laying.**

right: Jon Honeysett's friend and local historian, Maurice Young. He was celebrating his 11th birthday when the third Supermarine raid occurred – and attended the memorial service on his 71st.

far right: Mrs Joan Rolfe who laid a single rose in memory of her friend Margaret Moon who died on September 24, 1940 during the second Supermarine raid.

below right: Mr Ray Penny who lost his friend, 14-year-old "shop boy" Douglas Cruikshank, during the September 24 raid on Supermarine.

continued. Nonetheless, Hess's initiative failed and he was to spend the rest of his life in captivity until his apparent suicide in 1987. Other historians, convinced Hitler never intended to invade, buttress their arguments with statements of German generals made after the war. Field Marshall Rundstedt, for example, who was in command of the proposed invasion, told Allied investigators in 1945: "The proposed invasion was nonsense because adequate ships were not available – we looked upon the whole thing as a sort of game. I have a feeling the Fuehrer never really wanted to invade England. He definitely hoped the English would make peace."

Such accounts, offered in the atmosphere of the Nuremberg war crimes tribunal, have to be carefully re-examined. Many of Hitler's former aides thought it was in their best interests to now portray Hitler as a bumbling military buffoon. It was a strategy which some gambled would spare them from the hangman's noose. An overwhelming body of evidence – including mountainous secret German military files – continues to support the view that Hitler was in fact deadly serious about invasion. He wanted to do it. He would have done it. His main concern, however, was that a strategic precondition be fulfilled prior to invasion. Domination

of the skies – and hence obliteration of the RAF – had to be achieved before an amphibious landing of some 260,000 troops could be attempted across a 200-mile front stretching from Ramsgate to Lyme Bay.

Hitler could not invade for a number of complex, inter-related reasons. First and foremost, Goering's Luftwaffe could not destroy the RAF. Goering, Commander-in-Chief of the German Air Force, had boasted how his great aerial offensive would smash Britain within days. The total annihilation of

the RAF would take just a little longer – four weeks at most. To achieve his aerial Armageddon, he sent an average of 1,000 warplanes a day across the Channel from August 24–September 6. Yet his mighty Luftwaffe – massed into three giant "Luftflotten" fleets in Holland, France and Scandinavia – could not do it.

RAF Fighter Command, led by Air Chief Marshall Dowding, could muster only 620 Hurricanes and Spitfires at the outset in contrast to the Luftwaffe's compliment of 3,500.

Numbers aside, the respective aircraft on each side were, plane for plane, technically more or less even. They were broadly matched in armament, speed and manoeuvrability.

Hence it was ultimately the skills and bravery of RAF pilots – many between 18 and 20 years old - who decided the battle. Winning the battle was hardly the jolly, "tally-ho" jaunt that is so often portrayed in films. Far from it. Young people were thrown into a disorientating, terrifying environment where chances of survival only marginally improved once six missions were under their belts.

Secondly, Hitler's aerial supremacy could not be achieved because of key British support factors. The Royal Navy, for example, bolstered the psychological barrier presented by the Channel.

Britain also had a tremendous advantage in radar detection and in fighter control from the ground. The skill

right: **Tools of battle – the Hurricane and, below, the first production Spitfire photographed in May 1938 with Jeffrey Quill at the controls.**

of Fighter Command in committing its planes to battle against vastly superior forces was based on its shrewd use of radar. From the moment the Nazi planes took off from their European bases, they were picked up and the best attack positions determined. The Germans had no such comparable electronic aids and their military intelligence could not compensate. This category must also include the genius of Southampton's Reginald Mitchell and also Sydney Camm. They were the right men who designed the right aircraft – the Spitfire and Hurricane respectively – at precisely the right time.

Thirdly, Hitler's mistakes ensured his dream of aerial supremacy remained

September 1940. Five forward fighter fields in the South of England had been badly damaged and, far worse, six of the seven key sector RAF stations were so badly affected the whole communication system was on the verge of collapse. The scales, as Churchill wrote, had turned against Fighter Command.

Then on September 7, Hitler decided to switch his aerial attack away from airfields where the RAF was suffering and instead begin the bombardment of London, Southampton and main towns and cities. The reason has been previously explained: the unintentional bombing of London on August 25, 1940, had sparked RAF retaliation on Berlin. The German people had been assured their cities would never be hit. An angry Hitler now ordered his bombers to flatten British towns and cities – so granting the RAF's Hurricanes and Spitfires a reprieve at their airfields. Hitler effectively lost the Battle of Britain at this point – even though Southampton and London's Blitz terror was about to begin.

Fourthly, and most crucially, invasion failed to materialise because all the above factors combined to create increasing doubt and hesitancy within Hitler's mind about the feasibility of the operation. In turn, a general indecisiveness and uncertainty of priorities filtered right through the ranks. Hitler always viewed Operation Sea Lion as highly desirable but also as an "exceptionally bold and daring undertaking". His Navy and Air Force had also been cautious.

By October 1940, Hitler's lack of conviction had increased to the point where Sea Lion became more of a

elusive, and hence invasion rendered impossible. Prior to the Battle of Britain, he had already made one colossal blunder. On May 24, 1940, he halted German armoured divisions at Gravelines as they advanced on trapped British forces at Dunkirk therefore allowing the mass evacuation. Thirty thousand men were dead or missing, but more than 300,000 had escaped during the chaotic evacuation. Hitler, theoretically, had his best opportunity for invasion at this time but did not even attempt to establish localised air superiority over an invasion area.

Four months later, with RAF Fighter Command near breaking point due to sheer combat fatigue, Hitler blundered again. With bombed factories unable to replace lost Spitfires and Hurricanes, 176 aircrew killed during the August of 1940 alone and an inability to train new recruits quickly enough, the RAF was on the verge of being overwhelmed by

discussed concept than a focused, cohesive policy objective. The success of Britain's young pilots meanwhile convinced a dithering Hitler that invasion was impossible and on October 12, 1940, he effectively pulled the plug on the Sea Lion plan. The aerial phase of the Battle of Britain had been the first battle in history in which air power had played a principle role. Moreover, it was the first time in the war that Hitler had been checked.

If the fight in the skies had been lost, the sending of American bombers into fortress Britain would have been perilous if not impossible. The springboard for the whole D-Day assault on occupied Europe would have then been jeopardised. The aerial phase of the Battle of Britain was therefore one of the most decisive battles of the war as well as a classic defensive victory.

Now the Blitz phase of the Battle of Britain. The most obvious conclusion of the Blitz (September 1940 onwards) was that it demonstrated the acute limitation of air power as well as its capabilities. Both sides had crucially overestimated the "wearing down" effects of sustained bombing campaigns on infrastructure

and morale. Both sides also severely underestimated the sheer intensity of air power required to make bombing on this scale effective.

Hitler's attack on morale backfired. It was assumed by some that the civilian population would suffer a mass nervous breakdown. Philosopher Bertrand Russell predicted that London would be "one vast raving bedlam". The bombing would lead to rioting and the complete collapse of the social order. German psychiatrists agreed. They predicted mass hysteria in their own cities. They were all wrong. At the end of 1940, Hitler faced an enemy in Britain far more determined to fight than at the beginning of the year. Churchill described it as a "white glow, overpowering, sublime, which ran through our island from end to end".

These lessons of history, it could be argued, would not be learnt. The "Rolling Thunder" operation begun by American heavy bombers over North Vietnam in 1966 similarly failed. On President Johnson's orders, carrier-based jets hit every single road and rail bridge in the country as well as 4,000 of North Vietnam's 5,788 villages. About four million Vietnamese civilians – ten per

READERS RELIVE THE BLITZ

'Brave people made best of a bad job' AIR RAIDS 29/3/73

Did a blitz-hit Soton believe it was finished? 4/4/73

WAR-TORN SOTON IS DEFENDED 28 MAR 1973

'Council could not handle emergency' 27 MAR 1973

INDICTED: SOTON LEADERS IN BLITZ 27/3/73

Ordeal by bombing, 1940

'Almost a fanatic' condemned Soton's wartime town clerk 30/3/73

INDICTED: SOTON LEADERS IN BLITZ

BATTLE REOPENED
'Let's fight to clear our city's name'

cent of the population – were killed or injured during the conflict, yet still American victory could not be secured. While the country was physically damaged, the morale of the people was sufficiently not.

So what about the question of morale in Southampton during the bombing ordeal? The Inspector General of Air Raid Precautions, Wing Commander John Hodsoll, had visited the town shortly after the "Weekend Blitz" of November 30 – December 1, 1940. His conclusions, contained in a report to the Minister of Home Security, were not, to put it mildly, complimentary. He claimed that the local authority was incapable of dealing with the unfolding crisis and incapable of offering leadership. Indeed, some civic leaders were even accused of being more concerned about boarding trains out of the town to avoid the nightly bombing. Communication to the public and provision of information was also found wanting. Hodsoll noted that large numbers of residents had been leaving the town each night in anticipation of raids and had gone to the countryside for

safety. The government position on this practice ("trekking") was that it revealed weakness and lack of moral fibre. Consequently, no official assistance was offered to those leaving.

The government published Hodsoll's report in 1973 and Southampton erupted with fury. It hadn't helped that a month earlier the government had released another inflammatory 1940 report compiled by investigators from "Mass Observation", an independent organisation founded by sociologist Tom Harrison, which pioneered research into public opinion. The "Mass Observation" team claimed they had found a post-Blitz town where civilian morale had "distinctly deteriorated"; talk was obsessively dominated by discussion of the raids and was for many "dangerously near neurosis"; local resources and personalities were branded "inadequate"; and the strongest feeling of its inhabitants was that Southampton was "finished."

Such was the public outcry that a "Defence of Southampton Committee" was formed. Its own report answering the criticisms was later clipped to the Hodsoll

right: Nuremberg War Trials: Goering (front row of dock, far left with dark glasses and headphones) sits next to Rudolf Hess who now claimed to be suffering from amnesia. Hess and six former Nazis were sent to Berlin's Spandau Prison and these shuffling old men represented all that was left of the Nazi war machine. However was Hess, Prisoner Number Seven, really Hess? Many authors have claimed the Hess at Nuremberg was a double, the real Hess having been executed after his doomed arrival in Britain. Prisoner Number Seven was found hanging by an electrical flex in 1987 prompting theories he was murdered to prevent him spilling the beans should he be released. Others claim it was the real Hess in Spandau – but he was killed at the age of 93 to prevent him revealing embarrassing details of the peace discussions he conducted with Britain in 1941. Secrecy continues. The Hess files remain withheld and unavailable for public scrutiny.

Report which today rests in the Public Record Office. However, historians have since revisited the evidence and asked whether the "heroic" version of events should indeed be replaced by a more realistic, subjective and, ultimately, more accurate one. There were, claims this school, organisational mistakes, planning inefficiency, inadequate leadership and resulting morale problems. Maybe. Equally, however, difficulties remain, particularly when considering civilian morale. Moreover, they are difficulties which suggest that much academic analysis has been guilty of unfairness and insensitivity.

The key problem is the attempt to apply behaviour deemed desirable in a non-war environment to a situation in reverse. In short, is it valid to analyse 'normal behaviour' during times that were anything but normal?

There was no dress rehearsal for the Blitz, no trial run when the Southampton populous was invited to consider its reaction to the prospect of hundreds of tons of bombs being dumped upon it. Hence, amid the "Go To It" jingoism, resigned resolution, sangfroid atmosphere and pride in defying Hitler, there was

also anxiety, fear, anger, terror and panic. People were, in some cases, on the point of breaking. All extremes of human emotion naturally manifested themselves and merely matched the extreme experiences of the time. It was simply human nature to feel scared. "Trekking", therefore, was hardly cowardly – it was a basic survival instinct. All such responses were surely justified and understandable and, most importantly, wholly acceptable. Accusations of questionable leadership and planning incompetence must similarly be carefully justified when applied to an era of abnormal burdens and exceptional circumstances. Perhaps the critical failure was simply that planning was geared towards dealing with bombs and not coping with a traumatised, homeless population.

Moving on, certain human qualities are worthy of reflection during these unique times. There was, for example, humour and impressive resolve. After the "Blitz Weekend" of November 30/December 1, shops reopened with posters mocking and defying Hitler. In one newsagent's window was scrawled: "Hitler comes and goes but we go on for ever." A poster in a smashed photographer's declared: "Hitler's work is lousy – come and see ours!" Further along the street a shop's poster read: "You can't see our blasted windows –but we have stock inside!" All these shops had defiantly opened the very next day and customers simply clambered through smashed windows if the doors were blocked. There was also an abundance of courage exemplified by ambulance crews, firemen and Air Raid Precautions workers.

It is also important to note that countless men and women demonstrated they could lead two lives at once – their own jobs by day and aiding the war effort at night as wardens, Home Guard and fire personnel. The front line had come to them and, by and large, they met the challenge superbly well. Those serving in civil defence, fire and police services deserve fulsome praise as do those in the medical front line. They all displayed the highest standards of gallantry, courage and devotion to duty.

At this point, let's not forget the main players of this book – the children. The heroism of young people is easily overlooked. In fact they often proved more resilient than the adults. Teenagers manned the factories targeted by the Luftwaffe and youngsters helped the dying and injured as they lay in the streets. The children of the Blitz grew up quickly. Many were taught basic cooking and household chores at a young age and they helped fill the gap left by their serving fathers. They had to be equipped in case they would be left to fend for themselves and ended up making a vital contribution on the Home Front.

There are other, deeper perspectives to consider about the Blitz. Civilian bombing, as an instrument of war, demonstrated two extreme capabilities of human beings. On the one hand, the Blitz showed man at his most destructive, violent and unforgiving with childhood being sacrificed as part of wider goals. On the other, the Blitz showed our ability to adapt, survive and then rebuild in the most traumatic circumstances – a process achieved in Southampton as it was in Coventry and other towns and cities.

It is also important to remember the sacrifice made by German civilians. A heavy raid by 1940 standards was 100 tons of bombs, but later in the war the RAF and US Air Force were dropping

1,600 tons a night on Germany. In 1943, the Germans began to bear the full brunt of air warfare on a far more devastating scale than the Luftwaffe had dealt to others – even Londoners in 1940-41. Some 130 German towns and cities received heavy air attacks and the "Thunderclap" raid on Dresden in February 1945 caused a firestorm which left 80-110,000 killed or injured. Some 80,000 civilians may have died in Berlin too – more than the total for the whole of Britain. The German civilians, like the British, endured their ordeal bravely and stoically.

The bombing of Britain, meanwhile, curiously revealed another sobering facet of human nature: that acute adversity can foster a degree of human bonding which is apparently elusive in times of relative normality. The majority of contributors to this book fondly recall the Blitz "camaraderie and community spirit" coupled with the perception that "people would do anything for each other". Front doors "could be left open without fear of crime", too. While acknowledging that times were hard and emotionally damaging for many, they also fondly recall the simple pleasures of life in an age when the collection of car number plates and shrapnel constituted hobbies. While many contributors remember evacuation and the Blitz as times of anxiety and fear which robbed them of their childhood, equal numbers claim it was an "exciting upbringing", even "idyllic", and that it "set them up to cope with anything in life".

One consistent theme is the apparent demise, since the war, of community friendliness and camaraderie. These are aspects of 1940s life which, it is perceived, have mysteriously vanished in a discerning shift towards isolationism, greed and the general pursuit of self-interest. Contributors offer a range of opinions on the cause of this shift. These include the advent of television, which "replaced conversation and socialising and raised expectations"; the availability of money, which fostered greed and division among people; and greater educational opportunity, which created transient populations and changed the make-up of communities. Many believe the absence of money and expectations were great levellers which created a happiness in wartime that ironically waned in peacetime.

Contributors also lament the erosion of community pride. One said: "In my school, we were brought up to be proud of being a 'Northamite' and you certainly were. All the districts of Southampton were like that – there was this healthy, respectful pride and rivalry."

In-depth sociological research is required on the subject of perceived wartime bonding which, one hopes, would disprove the most obvious possibility of all: that it requires appalling conflict and a distinct and common enemy to bring out the collective best in us all. It may be that only extreme experiences like war can strip us of the unwelcome traits which otherwise surface and pollute life, such as greed and envy. What can then occur is a re-awakening of our most basic instincts and our most cherished desires – such as survival and the safety of our children.

Finally, it is worth adding that another consistent human trait once again surfaced during the Blitz period and proved instrumental in ensuring the survival of Southampton: man has an unnerving ability to make big mistakes. At yet another key juncture in the war, Hitler was to make another timely error. Following his poor judgement at the time of Dunkirk and his September 1940 gaffe which reprieved the RAF, he followed up nine months later with a decision to attack Russia. In June 1941, Hitler opened up a 2,000-mile front in the East and his aerial resources were diverted to support the new Operation Barbarossa. The Russian winter would prove to be Hitler's undoing while Southampton and his other premier British targets would be spared further bombardment. Hitler then declared war on America in December 1941 – yet another crucial blunder.

The costs of both the aerial and Blitz phases of the Battle of Britain must now be considered. By the end of October 1940, the Luftwaffe had lost about 1,800 aircraft and over 2,500 aircrew. The figures for Fighter Command were 1,100 aircraft lost and about 550 pilots killed.

The Blitz meanwhile had claimed hundreds of lives in Southampton among the 43,000 civilian fatalities in Britain during the air raids of 1940-41. That gruesome national toll included 5,500 children. More than 50,000 civilians were also seriously injured nationally (including 4,000 children) and over two million homes wrecked. A third of London had been razed while other targeted towns and cities had their own terrible tragedies – their own Supermarine, their own November 30th, their own Arts School equivalent. Add in the German civilian casualties and the full scale of the death of innocents reaches shattering proportions. Indeed, at the end of six years of war, Britain had suffered 60,595 civilian casualties and the Germans 600,000. The total estimated worldwide figure of civilian casualties is put at some 40 million.

Today, the memories of Southampton's survivors remind us of that time when the world went truly mad. They remind us of how a town suffered; they remind us of how a city was rebuilt; and, most importantly, they remind us of the strength of the human spirit. The children of the Blitz can today still tell the children of the new millennium what happened in 1940. When they no longer can, memories will slowly fade and recollections will dull. Time, in its carefree way, will ensure that once relevant history becomes slowly irrelevant.

However a number of memorial plaques will remain bolted and screwed to various spots around the city. The Art Gallery chamber exists as a shrine and the imposing Cenotaph will remind the forgetful. A heavy, gold-embossed book – entitled Roll of Honour of Civilian War Dead – is also tucked away inside the ornate Mayor's Reception Room at the Civic Centre. Then there is the white stone slab in Houndwell Place which goes largely unnoticed – a fact which helped to prompt this book. Memorials can connect the children of the future to the children of the Blitz. They can link the dazzling world of the Internet to the world of the blackout, sirens, bombing and carnage. When the connection is made, one message will be clear: a terrible sacrifice was made for their freedom.

Yet there may be another if they stay long enough to think: Love for the Blitz children inspired a town to fight, survive and ultimately triumph.

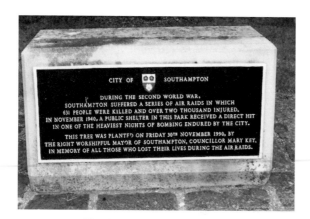

The Houndwell Place memorial
in Southampton.

THE END

CHAPTER 10

Selected contributors' biographies

The kind assistance of a considerable number of people made this book possible. Eighty men and women were interviewed as a means to weaving a tapestry of the times in which they grew up. They opened a door on a different era and painted a vivid, moving and fascinating picture of a particular snapshot in time. I am deeply indebted to each and every one of them.

Further, I sincerely hope the preceding pages represent a faithful reflection of the memories, views and information which they so generously offered.

A number of interviewees made a particularly significant contribution to the project. There follows a brief biography of some of these children of the Blitz which extends their stories from 1940 into the new millennium.

1. Al DONOVAN:
b. 23.3.31

The nine-year-old boy who saw Flt Lt James Nicolson bail out over Millbrook on August 16, 1940, left Regent's Park School in 1945. His varied career included two years in the Army, employment as a chef on the Mauretania liner, work at Fawley's Esso Refinery and a spell in Southampton Docks. Mr Donovan also worked at Mullards for 24 years (now Philips Semiconductors) which, curiously, was the location where Nicolson landed when the site was open land. He married Alma in 1952 and they have two children and three grandchildren. Mr and Mrs Donovan live in Southampton.

2. Olive RAMPTON (nee REYNOLDS):
b. 13.2.26

Fourteen-year-old Olive, who lost her parents in the Garibaldi pub bomb blast on November 23, 1940, left Bitterne Park School in 1939 and worked at Harrison's Dairy in Southampton. In 1968, she began a career spanning eighteen-and-a-half years with the Civil Service in Southampton. Olive married husband Charles in 1949 and they have three children and eight grandchildren. The Ramptons live in Wiltshire.

3. Janet WEBB (nee GROVES):
b. 5.8.38

The two-year-old girl who stood amid the wreckage of her Padwell Road home after a Heinkel bomber crashed in April 1941, left Western School in 1952. Her working life has included 28

years at the University of Southampton's Catering Department. Janet has one daughter and lives in Southampton.

4. Gwen HUGHES:
b. 17.5.11

Mrs Hughes and her two children, Gloria, five, and Anthony, two, were the only survivors when the Melbourne Restaurant shelter was hit during the raid of November 30, 1940. After the war, her husband Monty continued work as a fireman until he retired and a third child, Lynette, completed their family. Mrs Hughes was widowed in 1981. She lives in Southampton.

Daughter Gloria has recently retired from the Road Management System For Europe (ROMANSE) traffic project in Southampton. She is married, has two children and three grandchildren and lives in Southampton. Gloria says: "I can still vividly remember that night at the Melbourne. After the bomb fell I recall seeing the hand of my brother, Anthony, sticking out of the rubble before I was carried out. Then I remember the scene in the High Street. It was just a huge wall of fire."

Her brother Anthony is a chartered civil engineer. Mr Hughes is married, has three children and lives in Chandler's Ford.

5. Barbara BAKER (nee PARSONS):
b. 17.9.23

Barbara, who lost her father Jack when the Old Docks were bombed on September 26, 1940, left Clark's College in Southampton in 1939. She worked briefly for Southern Railway before marrying husband Donald and starting a family. They have one daughter,

two grandchildren and one great-grandson. Her husband founded the Mill Water Gardens in Romsey forty years ago.

6. Maurice YOUNG:
b. 26.9.29

The boy who watched the third

Supermarine raid on his 11th birthday went to work at White's Shipyard three years later where he started an apprenticeship as a boat and yacht builder. He later worked at Vosper Thornycroft as a loftsman. A keen diver who helped locate the Mary Rose wreck, Mr Young is today a local historian and researcher. He is married to Ann and they have three children.

7. Pat MALONE:
b. 25.8.29

The young evacuee came home from

Dorset at the age of 12 and returned to Northam Boys' School until he was 14. After National Service, Mr Malone became a train driver with Southern Railway. He has two daughters and is married to Patricia.

8. Ronald LYONS:
b. 7.8.32

Eight-year-old Ronald was hiding inside a pillbox in Chapel Road during the

Supermarine raid of September 26, 1940 when a baker's car was blown on top of it. After the war, Mr Lyons worked as a painter and decorator and as a bus conductor before spending two years in the

Army. A spell in the Merchant Navy followed before he entered Southampton Docks as a stevedore in 1954. He spent 25 years in the docks, continuing a family tradition of dock work which spans 100 years. Mr Lyons, who married Molly in 1954, lives in Southampton. They have five children, ten grandchildren and one great-grandchild.

9. Jack PARKER:
b. 19.3.27

Thirteen-year-old Jack lost his mother, two brothers and three sisters when

Melbourne Street was bombed on September 26, 1940. After the war, Mr Parker spent 48 years in the Merchant Navy – 37 of them as Captain of tankers. He married Jean in 1954 and they have two children and two grandchildren.

Mr and Mrs Parker have lived in Southampton all their lives.

Mr Parker's father died in 1961. His brother Ben, who survived the Melbourne Street bombing and wrote a poignant letter to his dad afterwards, went to sea after the war before joining the City Council's Refuse Department, where he was a supervisor. Ben Parker died in 1998 leaving wife Ruth and two sons.

Sister Rita (below), who escaped the bomb blast when she was sent on an errand moments earlier, married

American sailor Harold Kump and moved to America in 1946, aged 17. Her marriage lasted two years but she has remained in America ever since. She married Edwin Wells in 1949 and had three children but they were divorced in 1971. Her third marriage was to Myron Swope in 1975. Mr Swope died in 1981. Rita Swope now lives near Gettysburg, Pennsylvania, where she is an accountant

and interior designer. "I've had a wonderful full life in America ," she says. "But I still come back to see Southampton whenever I can."

10. Brenda PRITCHETT (nee LOGIE)

Southampton's teenage singer went on to work at Vickers, Hawker Siddeley and the Westminster Dredging Company. She started as a junior shorthand typist and became secretary/personal assistant to a director at Hawker Siddeley and a director at Westminster Dredging Company. Mrs Pritchett's singing career took off once more in 1984 when the City Council organised a commemorative "D-Day Plus 40" event. Mrs Pritchett - whose stage name is still Brenda Logie - is today the organiser of the "D-Singers" and is still busy giving evening performances. She is also part of a musical trio which gives afternoon shows.

11. Jean BARKER (nee Thorn):
b. 12.4.28

The 11-year-old evacuee who made a dash for freedom left Regent's Park School in 1944. She became a home help and

married husband Fred in 1950. They had seven children in ten years and now have eleven grandchildren and seven great-grandchildren. Mr and Mrs Barker live in Southampton.

12. Sam COOPER:
b. 7.9.25

Fifteen-year-old Sam was working as a cinema projectionist on November 30, 1940, the weekend of the main Blitz on Southampton. He left Millbrook School in 1939 and joined the Regal Cinema as a projectionist until he was 16. He then took up an apprenticeship with Folland Aircraft Company. Mr Cooper spent the rest of his working life in the aircraft industry interspersed with spells in both the Air Force and Army. He married Mary in 1956 and they have one child. They live in Wiltshire.

13. Ray MARTIN:
b. 9.2.38, and
Brian MARTIN:
b.30.7.34

One of Hitler's new V1 flying bombs landed less than 2 metres from where the young Martin brothers sat in their garden Anderson shelter in July 1944. After leaving Merry Oak School in 1953, Ray became an apprentice aircraft fitter at Hamble before embarking upon a career in engineering. He married Hazel in 1965 and they have two sons. They live in Southampton.

Older brother Brian left Merry Oak School in 1949 and joined an advertising firm for eight years. He then joined Ford Motors where he worked for 34 years. He married Margaret in 1960 and they have three children and two grandchildren. They live in Southampton.

14. Brian SIMPSON:
b. 9.8.30

The young armaments expert recalled walking past the Houndwell Park shelter, the scene of horrific carnage during the

"Blitz Weekend," when he was ten. At the age of 14, he started work at Vickers-Armstrong and two years later, in 1946, began an electrician's apprenticeship with the firm. At Eastleigh Airport, Brian worked on Spitfire Mark IXs for customers in Turkey and Belgium as part of a 12 year career spent in aircraft electrical work and building maintenance.

Mr Simpson has the distinction of being the last person to have completed the last job on the last Spitfire ever produced. On April 4, 1949, he fitted the radio and batteries to Mark 24 Spitfire VN 496, the last one made, before it flew off from Eastleigh towards South Stoneham Cemetery. Mr Simpson says: "In South Stoneham Cemetery lie the remains of R.J. Mitchell, the designer of the Spitfire, so perhaps it was fitting that the last Spitfire to be built flew over the grave of the man who gave us the greatest fighter plane in history. It was also appropriate that the last Spitfire of more than 20,000 produced should have flown off the same airfield as the first one – Number K5054 – which had made its maiden flight there 13 years previously on March 5, 1936."

Mr Simpson married Pam in 1951 and they have two daughters and three grandchildren. The Simpsons live in Dorset.

15. Lorraine POND (nee Longmore):
b. 13.6.46

At the age of 13, Lorraine was told by mother Joyce that her real father was an American GI, Robert Rateau, who had died six years earlier. Lorraine's mother had married Jack Longmore after the death of Mr Rateau in 1952 but they were divorced after 12

years. Joyce died in 1997.

Lorraine was shattered by the revelation about her real father and left the Millbrook family home in 1961. She moved to Buckie in Banffshire, north-east Scotland, to live with her stepfather Jack Longmore - the man she had believed was her real dad.

Lorraine returned to Southampton 18 months later and took up office work. Today, she works for Adams Morey at Redbridge, Southampton. She is also the well-known local singer of "Reflection Duo" which also features her partner. She has three children (the eldest of whom was named Robert after her American father) and five grandchildren.

16. Michael GLEDHILL:
b. 15.1.36

Four-year-old Michael and his six-year-old sister Veronica fled the Clarence pub with their mother on the night of November 30, 1940. Michael left Taunton's School in Highfield Road in 1954. Following two years national service, he became a merchant seaman and a chef before moving into the retirement home business. He married Valerie in 1968 and they have two children. The Gledhills live in Southampton.

Veronica (b. 17.4.39) left Deanery School in 1949 and worked in an off-licence before becoming a publican for much of her working life. In 1954, she married Bill Blow and had two children. Mrs Blow lives in Romsey. Michael and Veronica's father, Arthur - the manager of the Clarence pub who worked as an auxiliary fireman during the "Blitz Weekend" – died in February 1976. His wife died in 1988.

17: Harry GRIFFITHS:
b. 14.5.14

Mr Griffiths survived the raids on the Supermarine complex on September 24

and 26, 1940. He had joined the firm as a 14-year-old laboratory assistant (they were known as "handy lads") in 1928 and worked as part of the Design Department. Mr Griffiths worked at Supermarine for 34 years before joining the Deloro Stellite metallurgy company in Swindon where he became Technical Manager. He is widowed and has three children and four grandchildren.

18. Audrey HUNT:
b. 6.2.27

Thirteen-year-old Audrey was the only pupil from Central District Girls' School to survive the Luftwaffe bombing of the School of Art on November 6, 1940. She left hospital after treatment for burns and joined the Co-op in St Mary's, Southampton. Miss Hunt later worked for the Danish Baking Company in the New Docks before embarking upon an administrative career with the Independent Television Network which spanned 29 years.

19. Christabel LEIGHTON-PORTER:

The Eastleigh girl who achieved national fame as the model for the Daily Mirror's "Jane" died in December 2000.

The youngest of eleven children, her career did not take off until she was spotted by cartoonist Norman Pett who created the improbable secret agent, "Jane".

Christabel's curvaceous figure was Pett's inspiration for the cartoon-strip character who succeeded in losing most of her clothes during every adventure.

Idolised by the armed forces, she was shown nude in the Daily Mirror for the first time the day after D-Day.

The cartoon continued until 1959 when its heroine rowed off into the sunset with her sweetheart, Georgie.

Christabel's popularity saw her star first in a film," The Adventures of Jane" in 1950, and also in "The Jane Show" television series which ran until 1965.

Christabel then moved to Bermuda with her husband Arthur (a fighter pilot with 182 Typhoon Squadron which "Jane" adopted) and the couple stayed there for three years.

Christabel's career blossomed back home in Britain after she attended a Battle of Britain 40th anniversary event at Tangmere. She suddenly found herself in great demand again and personal appearances continued right up until her health began failing early in 2000 and she was diagnosed with cancer.

The Sussex-based Leighton-Porters had two children. Their daughter, Jane, was born in 1955 but died a few weeks later. They then had a son, Simon, now 43.

During her lifetime, Christabel revealed everything except her age which she described as '57 plus VAT.'

Her family finally gave up her best-kept secret after her death. She was 87.

Sources and recommended bibliography

Tim Clayton and Phil Craig, Finest Hour, Hodder and Stoughton, 1999

Malcolm Brown, Spitfire Summer, Carlton, 2000

Gordon Mitchell, R.J. Mitchell, Gordon Mitchell, 1986

Winston Ramsey, The Blitz Then and Now, Volumes One, Two and Three, After the Battle Publications, 1987-90

Albert Speer, Inside the Third Reich, Sphere, 1971

Hanson W. Baldwin, Battles Lost and Won, Robson Books, 2000

Peter Kilby, Southampton Through The Ages, CMP, 1997

Gordon Sewell, Echoes of a Century, Camelot Press, 1964

Roger Parkinson, Encyclopedia of Modern War, Routledge and Kegan Paul, 1977

Adrian Rance, Southampton: An Illustrated History, Milestone Publications, 1986

Brock McElheran, V-Bombs and Weathermaps, McGill-Queen's University Press, 1995

C.R. Russell, Spitfire Postscript, C.R. Russell, 1994

Matthew Parker, The Battle of Britain, Headline, 2000

H.R. Trevor-Roper, The Last Days of Hitler, Pan Books, 1983

William L. Shirer, The Rise and Fall of the Third Reich, Pan, 1964

Ben Wicks, No Time To Wave Goodbye, Bloomsbury, 1988

Tony Brode, The Southampton Blitz, Barry Shurlock, 1977

Peter Haining, The Day War Broke Out, W.H. Allen and Co., 1989

Albert Axell, Russia's heroes, 1941-45, Constable, 2001

Martin Gilbert, Finest Hour: Winston S. Churchill, 1939-41, (1989 edn) London, Heinemann 1994

Anthony Kemp, Southampton at War, 1939-45, Ensign Publications, 1989

Ingrid Peckham, Southampton and D-Day, Southampton City Council, 1994

Jon Honeysett, Death in the Afternoon, (unpublished), 1999

Bernard Knowles, Southampton: The

English Gateway, Hutchinson, 1951

Maurice Young, The Heinkel Crash (unpublished), 1999

Harry Griffiths, Testing Times, United Writers Publications, 1992

Robert Key, The Picture Post Album, Guild Publishing, 1989

Tom Hartman, Swastika at War, Leo Cooper, 1975

Frank and Joan Shaw, We Remember The Blitz, Hinkley, 1983

Claire Frankland, Donald Hyslop and Sheila Jemima, Southampton Blitz – The Unofficial Story, Oral History Team, Southampton Local Studies Section, Southampton City Council, 1990

Bob Carruthers and John Erickson, The Russian Front, Cassell, 1999

Robert Opie, The Wartime Scrapbook from Blitz to Victory 1939-1945, Narisa Chakra, 1995

Arthur Ward, The Battle of Britain, A Nation Alone, Chancellor Press, 1989

Alfred Price, Spitfire Story, Arms and Armour, 1999

Winston Churchill, The Second World War, two volumes, Cassell, 1948-9

John Keegan, The Second World War, Century Hutchinson, 1989

Laurence Thompson, 1940, Year of Legend, Year of History, London: William Collins 1966

The Southern Daily Echo Archives, Redbridge, Southampton

Ronald Atkin, Pillar of Fire: Dunkirk 1940, London: Sidgwick & Jackson, 1990

Hampshire, The County Magazine, Bedford Place, Southampton

Robert Kershaw: War Without Garlands. Operation Barbarossa 1941/42. Ian Allan, 2001

Lynn Picknett, Clive Prince and Stephen Prior, Double Standards. The Rudolf Hess Cover-up, Little, Brown and Company, 2001

Richard Holmes, Battlefields of the Second World War, BBC Worldwide Ltd, 2001

John Man, Atlas of D-Day, Penguin, 1994

Index

References including photographs are indicated by page numbers in **bold italics**